EAGLE EYE
and the
FALL *of* CREEK
CANYON

TED MOORE

ISBN
978-1-957895-44-4 (Paperback)
978-1-957895-43-7 (eBook)
978-1-957895-45-1 (Hardcover)

TABLE OF CONTENTS

CHAPTER ONE

The Telegram

"Crack!" The distinctive sound of a polo stick striking a wooden ball echoed off the nearby tree line on a warm summer day in 1871. Horses galloped, and people cheered and clapped for their teams. The beginning of the Victorian era brought forth a time when many people lived lavishly. Folks enjoyed outdoor sports such as croquet, baseball, and horseracing. During this prosperous time, residents in the small town of Saratoga, New York, made their living from tourism. Saratoga offered an assortment of inns, restaurants, shopping, and blacksmith shops. The upstate New York town even offered wagon-repair facilities to serve its visitors. One of the largest industries in Saratoga was the thoroughbred horse farms, which drew big business. The racehorse industry contributed to the town's prosperity as folks visited from all over the country. Saratoga's residents enjoyed other horse-related sports, including barrel racing and rodeos.

A man and his family lived in Saratoga, and they were members of the local country club, which stabled many of the finest purebred horses in the area. Richard DuFour was well liked by his neighbors and had an engineering degree specializing in factory layouts. He and his family enjoyed summer weekends at the club where they participated in popular outdoor sports. As a native French Canadian, Richard had attended college in Toronto, Canada, and also had earned additional chemical degrees in Albany, New York.

While at college, Richard was particularly good at playing polo and had competed in many polo tournaments in the area. Richard also was a firm believer in hunting and fishing to provide food and to help keep the wildlife population under control. Richard also enjoyed target practice with various styles of rifles and pistols, even though he wore thick glasses due to nearsightedness. A man with a slender build, Richard sported a short, clean haircut and maintained a thick, waxed mustache that curled up on each end, as was the style for gentlemen of the time.

One year when Richard was in Saratoga for one of his polo tournaments, he met the beautiful blond-haired, blue-eyed Pamela Dutcher. She was one of five siblings of the Dutcher family, which owned a horse ranch and bred some of the area's finest thoroughbreds. Richard and Pamela married and had a son. They named him Jonathan after Richard's grandfather but called him "Johnnie" for short. Little Johnnie displayed characteristics of both of his parents, having the brown eyes from his father's side and the blond hair from his mother's side. He was a well-mannered child, who enjoyed the company of other people. Along with doing well in school, Johnnie particularly enjoyed Bible studies in Sunday school. As a young lad, little Johnnie understood many of the teachings during the church services that followed the Sunday school classes.

Richard made a comfortable living as a factory engineer and often traveled from place to place, consulting with production companies. He specialized in steam-powered machinery and the manufacturing of nitroglycerine, a crucial ingredient in dynamite. Pamela ran the family's large Victorian home as an inn to provide lodging for travelers year-round. During the summer months, all of the inns in Saratoga were filled to capacity. During the winter months, however, only a few people braved the harsh weather to do some snowshoeing and cross-country skiing.

One day in August 1871, Richard was participating in a polo game at the country club. The ladies of the club, including Pamela, were enjoying each other's company decked out in their long-skirted gowns with an assortment of ruffles. The ladies also wore large, fancy hats to protect their porcelain white faces from the sun. Each fancy hat was secured with a large ribbon tied around the women's delicate chins. The cooks were roasting pork and beef outside on the hand-cranked rotisseries for a fine banquet when the games were through. On the field, Richard was up against some stiff competition. Near the end of the game, he reached down and scored the winning goal, making his team victorious. Pamela and the other women cheered the team's win. As Richard walked his horse to the stables, Johnnie came running up to him.

"Poppa! I saw you win! I saw it, Poppa, I saw you do it with my own two eyes!" Little Johnnie shouted.

"Yes, my son. But I couldn't have done it without the help from my teammates, you know," Richard said.

While Richard's horse drank water from the levy, he removed the sweating animal's saddle. Johnnie offered to take the saddle inside the stable.

"Can you handle it, my son?" Richard asked. "Sure can, Poppa!" Johnnie confidently replied.

Richard handed over the saddle. As Johnnie started to carry it, he and the saddle slowly dropped to the ground with an overwhelming "oof!" His father chuckled and offered the ten-year-old boy a hand.

"Wow, Poppa! I didn't know it was so heavy!" Johnnie said. "That's okay. We'll carry this thing in together."

Together they carried the saddle into the stable with Richard taking on most of its weight, allowing Johnnie to believe that he was doing the heavy lifting. After the pair finished putting away the gear, they wiped down the horse and led it to a stall. As Richard and Johnnie left the stable, they met up with the local messenger.

"Hate to bother you, sir, but I have a telegram for you," the man said. "Oh, that's okay, sir," replied Richard, laughing. "I get these all the time!" However, this was no ordinary telegram. The telegram was from the department of the United States government that dealt with settling the western frontier. The U.S. government had ongoing projects ranging from the expansion of the railroad systems to issuing land grants for farming. The government had also created an industrial movement program to help the United States expand, and it was this program that had sent the telegram. Richard read the small piece of paper with a puzzled expression.

TELEGRAPH
FROM: The Government of the United States of America
TO: Richard DuFour
SUBJECT: Your Expertise Is Required to Help Expand the West
PLEASE TAKE INTO CONSIDERATION THE FOLLOWING:
The temporary relocation of yourself and of your family
To work with engineers in developing copper
mines in South Dakota, United States
To aid in the construction of a nitroglycerine factory
You will receive a detailed letter soon.

"Is everything okay, Poppa?" asked the eager little boy.

"Everything will be fine, my son," Richard said.

Back at the house, Richard showed Pamela the telegram. She, too, seemed puzzled by the message. The couple discussed its contents, trying to make sense of it. Pamela had a feeling about what the telegram meant. Her uncle Nathan had taken part in the government's land grant program. Nathan had moved his family to Texas to start a beef cattle ranch. Pamela suspected that she and her family would soon be leaving the familiar home in upstate New York for the unsettled territories of the West.

The following day was Sunday, and Richard and his family prepared for worship services. The morning breakfast consisted of the usual Sunday treat of blueberry flapjacks, homemade sausage, and freshly squeezed orange juice, a rarity in those times. The family of three was quieter than usual, and Johnnie could feel the concern in the air.

"Mother? Poppa? Why are you so quiet?" Johnnie asked.

"Johnnie, my boy, we'll let you know if there's anything of your concern," Richard said. "Your mother and I just have some things to think about, that's all."

Johnnie knew that the telegram had something to do with this change of mood and figured his parents would eventually tell him about it. During Johnnie's Sunday school class, the group talked about having faith in God no matter what the circumstances are. The teacher used the story of the battle of Jericho and how the Israelites overtook the city as an example. In biblical times, God commanded the Israelites to march around the city of Jericho for six days and then retreat back to their camps. On the seventh day, God commanded the Israelites to march around Jericho seven times and wait for the next command. God then commanded them to blow their horns and shout out loud. When the Israelites obeyed God's command, Jericho's walls collapsed, and the Israelites overtook the city. Johnnie was quite intrigued with this story and couldn't wait to tell it to his parents.

After services, the DuFours rode to the horse farm to visit Pamela's father who was getting along in age and couldn't get around very well. At the Dutcher farm, Richard met Pamela's father, Joseph, in the smoking room, where they put on their smoking jackets to discuss business over their choice of smoke.

"Joseph, did Nathan find it difficult to move he and his family to Texas?" Richard asked.

"The only difficulty Nathan had was missing his relatives back home," Joseph said. "Otherwise, he was happy to make the move."

"I received a telegram myself asking me to make a move," Richard said. "But it will only be a temporary one."

"What does it entail?" Joseph asked.

"All the details aren't in the telegram, but I'll receive more information soon," Richard said.

"Well, Richard, all I know is that the government will usually aid you in your move if you choose to do so," Joseph said. "Let me know what additional information you find out."

"Indeed, I will," Richard replied.

Even though Richard didn't have all the details yet, he knew he was going to have to make a decision soon. Joseph also assured Richard that the government would grant them temporary land and, in his case, probably a house with an out-building.

The two men had just started to talk in more detail about how the program worked when a light knock came at the door. Joseph called out, "Enter!" and the door slowly opened. Johnnie was reluctant to disturb the men's discussion.

"Come on in, my boy!" Joseph said. "Why, don't be shy."

Johnnie had been talking with his mother and grandmother about the story of Jericho and the Israelites' faith. Johnnie asked his father if he remembered the story.

"Of course I do, son," Richard said with a laugh. "What do you think really caused the great walls of Jericho to tumble down?"

Johnnie thought for a minute and said, "Well, Poppa, God told the Israelites to march around the city one time for six days, and on the seventh day, to march around the city seven times."

"Okay, go on," Richard said.

"Well, on the seventh day, God's people shouted, beat their drums, and blew their horns until the walls fell down!" Johnnie said.

"Do you know what really caused the walls to collapse?" Richard asked Johnnie.

Johnnie thought for a moment and said, "Well, when the Israelites did what God told them to do, the noise of all of them shouting and blowing their horns made the walls crumble. Right?"

"Well, yes and no," Richard said.

"You see, my son, the faith of the Israelites doing what the Lord commanded, whether it seemed silly or not, brought the walls down. The shouting and trumpet blowing itself had nothing to do with Jericho's walls collapsing."

Johnnie's face brightened as he understood better what it meant to have faith in the Lord.

In the dining room, the women sipped tea while they discussed the week's events around town. They also exchanged news about other family members, including Nathan and his beef cattle ranch in Texas. The Dutcher family's two maids were preparing the evening meal while the women waited for Pamela's other siblings to join them. As the day wore on, the family members in the area, with the exception of Pamela's oldest brother, Joseph Jr., who lived in Yonkers, New York, arrived at the family horse farm. When everyone had arrived, they played yard games with the children before sitting down to eat at the enormous dining room table.

When evening had arrived, the Dutcher family sat down around the table to discuss business. Richard, Joseph, and Pamela didn't mention the recent telegram. There was laughter, storytelling, and sampling of good apple pie as the families joined together in harmony. The Dutcher family also enjoyed hearing Pamela's niece play the violin.

In the late evening, the family members had to light the lanterns mounted to their carriages for the journey home. When Richard and his family arrived at their Victorian home, the caretaker assured them all was well and the guests staying there that weekend were comfortable as well. Richard thanked their trusted caretaker for watching over things. After putting Johnnie to bed, Richard and Pamela laid awake for a while pondering what the future held.

"What could this mean for our future, Pamela?" Richard asked. "Would it open more doors of opportunity for my line of work?"

"What about the inn?" Pamela asked. "We must not forget about our son's future either."

"I know, my love. We may have much to consider very soon," Richard said. Soon they both drifted off to sleep. The new week started out as any other normal week. Pamela, the inn's maids, and the housekeepers tended to their visitors' needs. Richard reported to his office in town to deal with the distribution of chemicals to various industries. Johnnie's day included helping out around the house with chores.

On Wednesday, while Richard was in his office, a large envelope arrived for him from Washington DC. It was the long-awaited information concerning the government's request for his expertise in factory systems and chemicals. Curious, Richard tore open the envelope and began reading its contents. The paperwork described an ideal mining area in South Dakota for copper. The letter called for the completion of a very large nitroglycerine plant called the Creek Canyon Chemical Company that would produce not only nitroglycerine, but also other main ingredients for the production of dynamite.

This plant would be the largest factory of its type in the country and perhaps in the world. The nitro plant was located in the small town of Creek Canyon, South Dakota, which was strictly a mining town. The government wanted Richard to oversee the steam pipe construction of the plant for a season and to monitor the fabrication of its ironworks. Richard's main responsibility would be to supervise the layout of the plant's systems to make sure everything would operate safely. Richard was also asked to educate the workers not only about how to operate the plant's systems and safety issues, but also about the proper use of the chemicals involved in its processes. He was given two weeks to respond to the government's office via telegram to let them know his decision.

That evening, Richard showed his wife the letter. Pamela was sympathetic toward her husband's need to help others. The trip west would be the longest time Richard would be away from home. The government had requested about three months of his services on this particular project. Even though Pamela didn't know much about the industrial movement of the country, she knew it was important to her husband and possibly to their son's future. Richard knew his position as an engineer in Saratoga wouldn't be affected because traveling was part of his line of work.

"The government assures me that they are willing to pay for you and Jonathan to make the trip as well," Richard told Pamela. "They will also have a home set up for us upon our arrival in Creek Canyon."

"Shall we have someone oversee the inn while we are away?" Pamela asked. "Who do you suppose will do such a thing if something should happen to us?"

"How about your sister, Deborah?" Richard asked. "I'm sure she and her family would be able to handle the inn."

"Marvelous idea, my dear husband!" Pamela said. "We also need to think about Jonathan's schooling as well while we're out West."

"Yes, indeed we do," Richard replied. "The schooling may not be as favorable as it is here."

"I know," Pamela said. "But if Jonathan falls somewhat behind out in South Dakota, I'm sure he'll regain himself when we return. After all, he's a bright boy."

"Yes, he is," Richard said. "So let's take this opportunity and hope for the best."

"Okay, Richard. But let's wait until Saturday to tell Jonathan and the servants," Pamela said.

"Very well, my love. We'll inform them on Saturday."

Saturday arrived with claps of thunder and flashes of lightning along with a heavy rain. Richard and Pamela sat down with the servants and also with Johnnie to tell them what they had been thinking about since the telegram's arrival. Johnnie and the servants understood how hard it was for Richard to make his decision. Then the servants were amazed that Richard wanted his family to make the long journey by train to South Dakota with him. Johnnie didn't seem to mind this idea because it would be a whole new adventure for him, and he would be away from his usual days of schooling.

Sunday arrived with a crisp feel in the air and the birds singing outside. The sunshine was bright after the long, hard rains since Friday. This time, the feeling in the air was one of excitement as the DuFours ate the weekly blueberry flapjacks and drank freshly squeezed orange juice. They went to church services and enjoyed the teachings along with the congregational singing. After services, Richard invited Pamela's family to meet at their favorite restaurant in town to eat and discuss matters concerning their decision to head out West. Deborah and her husband, Anthony, agreed to oversee the inn with the help from their two children. Everyone supported Richard, Pamela, and Johnnie and wished them well on their journey that was to take place within a few weeks.

On Monday, when Richard returned to work, he sent a telegram to Washington DC to let the government know his decision. Richard received a telegram back telling him to stop at an office located in Queens, New York, to pick up drawings of the layout of the plant and the hydro dam that would provide the waterpower for the plant's operations.

CHAPTER TWO

Richard's Haunting Experience

The following weeks went by more quickly than the DuFour family expected. It was the middle of September, and all the preparations had been made for Deborah and her family to take charge of the Victoria Inn. The DuFours had been packing their personal belongings in traveling trunks. Most of what they were taking with them was clothing, but some boxes contained jewelry, currency, and eating utensils. Other cases contained some fine china and a couple of pistols from Richard's gun collection with plenty of ammunition. Johnnie had some hand-carved figurine toys one of the caretakers had whittled for him from willow wood. He was also taking along a small die-cast train set his parents had given him for Christmas one year and had managed to pack the stickball set he and his friends played with during the summer months.

The day before the big trip was to begin, the DuFour family gathered everything they were going to take, and loaded up the carriage that would take them and their luggage to the train station in Saratoga. That evening, the DuFours and the Dutchers had their last family gathering to celebrate the journey that would begin the next morning. The two families enjoyed a nice meal at the inn and sang some songs. The children played instruments and danced. After the cozy festivities, the two families gathered in prayer to ask the Lord for guidance for the DuFours' travels. Then the families tearfully exchanged good-byes.

"Have a safe travel," Deborah said to Richard, Pamela, and little Johnnie with tears in her eyes.

"May the Lord watch over all of you," Joseph said.

Pamela exchanged tearful hugs with her family, and Richard shook hands all around, and they parted ways with well wishes. When Saturday, September 25th arrived, the DuFours and the inn's employees gathered around the breakfast table for one last blueberry flapjack breakfast. Little was said because everyone was anxious about the train ride that would begin in a couple of hours. After the meal was completed and the table cleared, it was time to board the carriage and head into town. The staff gave long, warm hugs to the DuFours and wished them well.

The family of three arrived at the train station on time and, with the help of the carriage driver, unloaded the luggage. The train's conductors loaded the DuFours' belongings on the train while Richard sent a telegram to New York City. When he rejoined his family, Richard pulled out the tickets from his pocket and handed them to Pamela and Johnnie.

"All aboard!" the conductor yelled.

"Oh boy! Here we go!" Johnnie said.

Richard smiled at his son. "Are you ready to start the first journey of your life, son?'

"Sure thing, Poppa!" Johnnie shouted out as he boarded the train.

Richard and his family sat down in one of the train's coaches, and not long after the passengers had boarded, the loud whistle blew, causing Johnnie to jump in his seat. The steam engines slowly started to push the large drive wheels of the train. Steam shot out of one side of the engine with a loud chug and then out of the other side with the same loud chug. As the train picked up speed, the chugging from the steam engine grew faster and faster.

"How does the engine work, Poppa?" Johnnie asked.

Richard happily explained to his son the mechanics of the train's engine.

"Well, son, the train uses coal from the coal car to feed its big iron boilers and keep the water hot, producing the steam power needed to operate the train. The inside of the engine has parts called pistons that are shaped sort of like barrels," Richard added.

Johnnie wrinkled his forehead. "What do those pistons do?" he asked.

Richard chuckled a bit and said, "The pistons slide up and down inside the engine from the pressure of the steam and are connected to those big rods on the wheels. When one piston is pushing, the other one is pulling in steam, getting ready to push also."

"Wow, Poppa, you know a lot of things!" Johnnie said.

Pamela smiled as she listened to the conversation between her husband and son. The train ride south was not as smooth as it looked from the outside. The train's coach seats grew uncomfortable after a while, and the train cars rocked back and forth vigorously. The cars seemed to buck up and down as the train traveled down the tracks with a clackety-clack, clackety-clack. The train made stops on its way to New York City, with Albany, New York, being the first. Richard and his family were grateful for the chance to get out of the coach and walk around a bit to stretch their legs and give their butts a break from sitting on the hard wooden seats. The family did this at every stop as they proceeded south to Grand Central Station in New York City. The DuFours ate in the train's dining car, and even though the food was not as good as home cooking, it held their stomachs over during the long trip.

At the train station in Poughkeepsie, New York, Pamela wired her brother, Joseph Jr., concerning their time of arrival at Grand Central Station. Joseph Jr. would arrange to pick up the DuFours and take them back to his house, where the family would stay the night. Pamela hadn't seen her brother and his family in a couple of years.

The train arrived at Grand Central Station on time. Inside the station, Johnnie looked around in amazement at the station's high ceilings and magnificent architecture. Joseph Jr. spotted Pamela and yelled out, "Pamela, Pamela!"

His voice echoed around the station. The two families greeted each other with open arms and hugs and kisses. They loaded the luggage and climbed inside Joseph Jr.'s carriage to make their way into Queens to pick up the drawings, which would help Richard understand the project in further detail. The DuFours made it to the office a half hour before it closed for the day.

When the DuFours arrived at Joseph Jr.'s place, Pamela's sister-in-law, Rachel, and her two sons, William and Robert, shook their relatives' hands, trying to act like little gentlemen. Everyone helped unload the luggage and put it in a spare room. The smell of good food reminded the DuFours of home. The two families sat down and ate an enjoyable meal and shared stories.

"My sister. If life isn't hard enough in your area, will it not be even tougher in the wild west of South Dakota?" Joseph Jr. asked.

"Life will indeed be harder in South Dakota, but luckily, we aren't going to spend the whole winter there," Pamela said.

The two families were curious about what was in the two leather tubes Richard had picked up in Queens. Everyone gathered around the dining room table, and Richard opened up one of the tubes. He pulled out the large, rolled-up piece of thick paper, and the two families helped him slowly unroll the drawing of the layout of the nitroglycerine processing plant. Richard explained how the boilers operated and how the steam pipes distributed the steam power through the iron pipelines to different sections of the facility.

"These pipes provide steam power to the machines for productions in the plant," Richard said as he moved his finger along the drawing. "The rest of the steam is let off into the air through the exhaust stacks outside."

"Poppa, you mean sort of like the train engine?" Johnnie asked. "Exactly, my son! Good observation!" Richard said proudly.

Richard went on to explain how nitroglycerine is produced and how the steam-powered machines play a part in the process.

"Let's open this one up!" William said excitedly, pointing at the other tube. "Now, now, son, mind your manners," Joseph Jr. said, a little embarrassed. "That's alright," Richard assured him. "He means no harm."

William handed Richard the second tube. Once again, everyone helped Richard unroll the second drawing. This drawing, however, was of a very large stone hydro dam erected several years earlier to provide waterpower for various mining operations. Some of the water wheels drove equipment to grind minerals into powders that would be combined at the nitroglycerine facility to make dynamite and other explosives such as gunpowder. Other water wheels were used for conveyor systems that moved rock and dirt to sift out the copper ore.

As Richard peered at the drawing of the dam, a sudden feeling of darkness fell over him. Richard stood silently for a moment and then started feeling a little queasy.

"Are you alright?" Pamela asked.

Richard nodded his head. "I think so," he said. "I mean, all of a sudden, I felt like some sort of a spell came over me."

Pamela felt his forehead. "Do you feel ill?" she asked.

"No, not really," Richard said.

"What was it like?" Joseph Jr. asked.

"Well, I don't know. It was like some sort of wave of depression or something," Richard said.

"Do you think there's something wrong with the dam's structure?" Rachel asked.

"As far as I can see, the dam itself looks perfectly safe," Richard said.

"What do you think is the matter, Poppa?" Johnnie asked.

"Well, I'm not quite sure right now, son," Richard said.

"I think we should play a card game or something." Pamela said, breaking the silence. "We had a rather tiring trip down."

"You may be right, my sister," Rachel said. "Perhaps we should just relax a bit and enjoy one another's company for the rest of the evening."

"Yes indeed, my love," Joseph Jr. said.

The two families ate some pie and played a few card games under the light of the oil lamps. After a couple hours, it was time to turn in for the night. Pamela fell asleep rather quickly, but Richard remained awake for a while, wondering why he felt the way he did about the hydro dam's diagram. Richard slowly drifted off to sleep and slept well until morning.

The next morning, the smell of bacon and eggs filled the house. The families met in the dining room for a hearty morning meal. As the two families ate together, they discussed the day's events for after Sunday worship services.

Johnnie was eager to see what his uncle's congregation was like and couldn't wait to get to the church. Joseph Jr. had arranged for a large, horse-drawn carriage taxi service to pick up the two families and drive them to worship services so they could all ride together.

The Sunday school classes were much larger than the ones in Saratoga. When the teacher asked questions about what they learned that day, little Johnnie answered several correctly. The Sunday school teacher was amazed at Johnnie's attentiveness. The church services were much larger as well, and the building with its cathedral ceilings had great acoustics for the preacher. The singing was loud and magnificent, filling the building with joyous hymns. After the services, Joseph Jr. introduced Richard and his family to the preacher.

"Reverend? This is my brother-in-law Richard DuFour and his wife, my sister Pamela," Joseph Jr. said. "And, oh yes! Their delightful and handsome son, Jonathan."

After shaking hands with the preacher, Joseph Jr. introduced the DuFours to some of the congregation's elders. Johnnie was especially pleased to greet them with his firm little handshake. The men of the church were delighted at the fine young man Johnnie was growing up to be.

After the families had finished socializing, the horse-drawn carriage taxi arrived to take them to their next destination. The day was warm and sunny, so they decided to eat lunch at a nearby restaurant and then proceed to Central Park in another hired taxi with an open top. The day was a splendid one as the families played outdoor games with other people in the park.

The park itself was beautiful to walk around in and gave the families a chance to observe different birds that made the park their home. When everyone was tired from all the activities, they returned to Joseph Jr.'s house to partake of the meal the servants had prepared for them. Dinner was very filling, and the two families planned to retire early enough to get a good night's sleep. Richard, Pamela, and Johnnie had to get on the morning train to continue their journey, and Joseph Jr. had to return to his job as a store manager at the Macy's store.

Before the two families retired for the night, they sat down for dessert: blueberry muffins and tea for the women and children, and coffee along with a smoke for the men. The blueberry muffins reminded Johnnie of the blueberry flapjacks back home. Everyone talked about the journey ahead for Richard and Pamela.

"I'll keep in contact with you, my brother, through the telegram system," Pamela said.

The DuFours got up from the table to start putting away their clothes and personal belongings so their trunks could be loaded onto the carriage the next morning. The last items to be put away were the two drawings in the leather tubes. Joseph Jr. picked up the one with the nitroglycerine plant layout in it. As Richard picked up the one containing the drawing of the hydro dam, both men looked at each other.

"What shall we do with that one?" Joseph Jr. asked. "Shall we take another look at the drawing?"

The women and children gathered around the table as the two men stared at one another.

Richard spoke up. "Joseph, will you give me a hand with this once again?" "Sure thing, my brother." Joseph Jr. said. "Sure thing."

The two men slowly pulled out the drawing of the dam a second time, and as the women and children looked on silently, Richard and Joseph Jr. spread the sketch on the dining room table. Not knowing what to expect this time, Richard's heart pounded and his hands trembled. As he and his brother-in-law held the drawing open, Richard stared at it. As he stood there glaring at the paper, the room's lighting seemed to grow very dim. Richard blinked several times to try to refocus on what he was looking at. The same feeling of depression fell over him once again like a blanket. The others noticed the change that had come over Richard.

"Do you need to stop looking at the sketch?" Pamela asked.

"No!" Richard said with a tremble in his voice. "I must find out what this thing is all about."

As Richard stared at the drawing intently, he heard something in his head. He heard faint, ghostly cries of anguish.

"What can this be?" Richard whispered. "What can this be?"

The women and children were frightened by what they saw in Richard's face as he stood there shaking, still peering at the diagram.

"Do you want to stop, Richard?" Joseph Jr. asked.

"No, no, no. I must find out what this is all about!" Richard said as he began to sweat profusely.

After a few minutes, Richard began to calm down. He was determined to let the haunting experience run its course. The feeling of sadness persisted, and Richard could still hear the faint cries and screaming. After a while, the sounds faded away, and the feeling of depression slowly lifted. With a big sigh of relief, Richard wiped the sweat off his brow, face, and neck as his emotions returned to normal.

"Well, dear? Are you feeling better now?" Pamela asked with a look of concern flooding her face.

"Yes, I do," Richard said, relieved.

"What do you think it was all about, Richard?" Joseph Jr. asked.

"Well, I don't know right now, but I'm sure I'll find out," Richard said.

"Meanwhile, I will pray to God for answers, and I won't open this tube again until I see the dam myself."

With that said, both families turned in for the night. Monday morning arrived with a mist in the air and the skies gloomy and overcast. The two families were quiet as they ate their final breakfast together before parting ways. Rachel and the children hugged Richard's family and wished them well. The DuFours boarded Joseph's carriage for the trip to the train station. The horse and buggy arrived at Grand Central Station, where the DuFour family would board the New York Central Railroad Company train to begin their long journey westward.

"Good-bye, my brother!" Pamela sobbed as she hugged and kissed him.

"May only good things happen to you all," Joseph Jr. said as he shook hands with Richard and Johnnie.

Pamela shed some tears as she watched her eldest brother drive away in his carriage.

CHAPTER THREE
The Journey Westward

The train Richard's family boarded at Grand Central Station was quite a bit larger than the one they had taken from Saratoga. This time, the train's engine had three large drive wheels on each side, instead of two like the previous one. The train's cars were also larger, longer, and heavier, which made them more comfortable to ride in. The seats were of padded leather, which cushioned the bumps sent up through the floor from the tracks.

The next stop was Pittsburgh, Pennsylvania. When the train arrived in Pittsburgh, the DuFours got off the train to eat lunch in a tavern recommended by a passenger they had made acquaintances with. The layover was two hours long for greasing and oiling. Because Pittsburgh was a steel-industry town, Richard had a friend in the business whom he had visited during one of his engineering trips.

The previous year, Richard had consulted with some employees at this friend's factory about a more efficient way to produce steel. The company had taken an interest in the production of steel I-beams. Richard helped coordinate the proper processes for the company to make a stronger steel alloy. Now Myron Smith, who ran the facility, welcomed Richard and his family to the factory.

"Good day, my fellow companion!" Myron said. "The processes you taught us were very helpful with our success!"

"Good day to you, too, my man!" Richard said with a smile.

"Since your last visit, sales are up due to the construction industry's use of steel-reinforced brick walls," Myron said. "Now, larger buildings within our rapidly growing town can be constructed with this new method."

Myron and the DuFours toured the plant. Johnnie was intrigued by the massive smelting pots overflowing with red-hot molten metal. The young boy was also amazed at how the soft red-hot steel bars were formed into I-beams. After the tour, the two men parted with a handshake, and Myron exchanged well wishes with Pamela and Johnnie. Back at the station, the Pennsylvania Railroad Company had the train loaded up with coal, and its water tank was topped off. The DuFours were ready to roll once again! As they started their trip toward Cincinnati, Ohio, Johnnie and his father discussed the use of steel beams.

"You see, son, by making steel beams longer and stronger, we can make buildings taller than ever," Richard said. "First, they build a skeleton for a tall building much like a skeleton in our bodies. Then they fill in the rest of the walls with bricks."

Johnnie listened intently while his father talked about the uses of steel. The Pennsylvania train made its scheduled stops, and the DuFour family got off the train in Columbus, Ohio, to dine in town while the train was restocked with coal and water. This time, the layover wasn't as long because the train didn't need as much maintenance as it had in Pittsburgh. After the DuFours finished their meal, they hurried back to the station to board the train once again. Their final destination that night was Cincinnati, Ohio.

The train ride was long and tiresome as they approached their next stop. Even though the seats were more comfortable, sitting in one position for any length of time numbed their legs and buttocks. Johnnie had to switch sitting positions often to try to keep comfortable. When the DuFours arrived in Cincinnati, they checked in at a nearby inn for the night. The following morning would leave Richard and his family little time for breakfast before they had to board a train owned by yet another railroad company. The multiple and sometimes confusing process of switching train companies was a pattern throughout the trip.

The inn was comfortable, and as soon as they dropped their luggage on the floor, the DuFours dressed in their nightclothes and climbed into bed. The weary family was sound asleep within minutes. The next morning brought the sounds of the hustle and bustle of city streets. The DuFours rose out of bed, got dressed, and ventured outside. The first thing they noticed was the massive amounts of carriages traveling up and down the street. Stagecoaches were transporting people, and horse-drawn wagons were transporting all sorts of materials, such as wooden barrels, lumber, and an assortment of feedbags.

Then, all of a sudden, a loud "Bang! Bang!" came from down the street. Little Johnnie ran and ducked behind a parked buggy; he thought the noise was gunfire. The noise also startled Richard and Pamela. The family peered down the street and saw a funny-looking contraption mounted on top of a cart. It had a cylinder that sat sideways and was connected to two steel wheels. One end of a large belt was attached to one of its wheels, and the other end of the belt was running some type of machine. Johnnie was amazed to see this odd-looking thing and looked at his father with a quizzical expression.

Richard looked at Johnnie and shouted, "Ah! It's one of those new internal combustion engines!"

"An internal what?" Johnnie asked.

"A type of engine that uses a fuel called gasoline instead of steam," his father said. "Some people use them to power equipment with a large belt like this one."

The DuFours and others on the street watched with amazement as this engine demonstrated its power with sort of a loud putt-putt sound coming from it. Not only did the oddity make a lot of noise, but also it gave off a black, smelly smoke that rose above it. The large belt attached to the gasoline engine was powering a machine that stripped corn kernels off of the cobs. Richard tried to explain how a gasoline internal combustion engine worked to Pamela and Johnnie. Richard used the way the train's steam engine worked as an example.

"You see, instead of using fire to heat water to push steam *into* the engine, the gasoline engine explodes the gasoline inside of itself to push hot smoke *out* of the engine," Richard said. "It's just a different way to produce power."

"Do you think everybody will have one of those?" Johnnie asked.

"Well, I don't know," his father answered with a laugh. "It's sort of a novelty thing with farmers right now."

While Richard and his family watched the machine, they heard the train's boarding whistle blow and knew it was time to continue their journey to Chicago, Illinois. Their next major stop would be Indianapolis, Indiana.

On the way to Indiana, the three of them had a lively discussion about what they were seeing and experiencing. The change of scenery was pleasant, but never in her life did Pamela ever think she would take an interest in the things that would change the industrial world. Pamela always thought that the inn or the horse business would secure a future. Now, she started to realize that people would have to make changes to keep up with what the country was experiencing. Pamela was pleased to see her son taking an interest in his father's knowledge.

Before the DuFours knew it, the train had started to slow down. They were nearing Indianapolis, and Richard and his family planned to get lunch somewhere in town. The DuFours wondered what experiences this city would offer. What the DuFours didn't realize was that September was the time of year for bad thunderstorms, usually accompanied by large, destructive hail. The afternoon air was hot and still as the DuFours looked for a place to rest and eat.

As the three of them strolled down the streets of Indianapolis, Johnnie noticed a few odd-looking devices. They were like small fans mounted on top of iron posts ranging from six to eight feet in height. They had rudders on the back of the fan housings, like a weather vane indicating wind direction by swiveling. The strangest thing of all about these devices was that they had a cylindrical object attached to the rear part of the fans. Johnnie pointed to one of fan-like objects and asked his father, "What are those things for, Poppa?"

Richard, bewildered at what he saw, looked at Johnnie and said, "You know, my son? I haven't the foggiest!"

For the first time ever, Richard couldn't answer one of Johnnie's questions. Little Johnnie looked up at his father with a smile and walked next to him. The DuFour family came upon a fine-dining restaurant, and as part of their tradition, they sampled some of the different types of foods offered by the area people. The DuFours tried some pork tenderloins and some of Indiana's finest vegetables and potatoes from local farmers. Pamela noticed the Midwesterners' fancy dresses were a little subtler than those back home in upstate New York. The dresses had less lace-work, and the hats were a little smaller too. While they were eating and observing those around them, the DuFours noticed the sun had disappeared.

"We might be in for a little rain," Pamela said to her family.

Within moments, the restaurant began growing darker and darker. After a minute or two, Richard said, "Heck, we might be in for a lot of rain!"

A nearby patron overheard Richard and looked straight at him. "Mister, we might be in for a tornado!"

The others in the dining area quieted as the sky grew even darker. The wind started to pick up, and the tree leaves rustled loudly as the wind blew them in all directions. Then came the sound of a stone hitting a tin roof. After that came another and then another. Before everyone knew it, the sky let loose a mighty rush of marble-sized hailstones, pelting everything in sight! The horses outside thrashed around in fright, and their riders were bucked off. Some horses pulling wagons ran wildly through the streets, dispersing cargo everywhere.

Then came the pouring rain! The rain blew down from the sky so fiercely it looked like walls of water moving down the streets. Men, women, and children rushed to find any shelter they could. People soaked by the heavy rain even rushed into the restaurant. It only took seconds for anyone who happened to be in the streets to be drenched from head to toe. The marble-sized hail hitting the buildings' tin roofs sounded like fierce gunfire to Johnnie's ears! People yelled and called out to one another as they gathered together to ride out the storm. Some of the horses had to be cut loose from hitching posts to keep them from panicking in the streets, while those tied to wagons had to be quickly freed.

Little Johnnie was so frightened that he hid under the table. Johnnie had seen thunderstorms with pea-sized hail back home, but he had never seen a storm of this magnitude. The street, dry and dusty only ten minutes ago, now seemed to be a river of mud! As it continued to rain, people trying to cross the street slipped and slid in the mud, falling in the middle of the street.

After about fifteen minutes or so, the rain stopped as quickly as it had started. The sky was still very dark, though, and even had an eerie dark greenish color to it. The wind also had momentarily stopped blowing. Richard said to his family, "Come on! Let's make a run for the train station!"

The three darted out the door before anyone could warn them not to, and they made their way to the station. As they drew near the station, the DuFours heard what sounded like a train pulling away. At first, they thought their train had left them behind with their luggage on board. Then they realized the sound they heard was growing even louder and louder. The conductor pointed behind them and yelled, "*Tornado*!" The DuFours spun around and saw a twister headed right for the city! The large black funnel cloud wobbled back and forth like a giant, squirming snake!

As the fierce wind picked up, the DuFours heard the whirling siren sounds coming from the weird-looking fan-like objects. When the wind shifted, the fans spun around according to the direction of the wind while the sirens got louder and louder. As the twister drew closer, the fans spun faster and changed directions more violently. The conductor yelled to Richard and his family to seek shelter in a nearby storm cellar. The three terrified upstate New Yorkers did as they were told and took shelter to ride out the oncoming tornado. While in the storm cellar, the DuFours could hear the roaring wind outside. It was louder than any train they had ever heard. The storm cellar doors shuddered violently, and everyone inside thought the doors would be torn off.

"My goodness, man!" Richard said to the conductor. "Does this happen very often?"

"Well, yes, but not always in the same place," the conductor said.

"You mean to tell me that this sort of thing can happen at any time, anywhere?" Richard shouted.

"Yes, but mostly in the spring and late-summer months," the conductor said.

Outside, debris was flying everywhere! Trees and large limbs were crashing on top of buildings as the violent twister flung them around. Debris from already-destroyed buildings was strewn all over the place like matchsticks, along with whatever contents had been inside the buildings. Wagons were lifted like toys and smashed back down into the streets and sometimes even right through house roofs! Wheels from some of the smashed wagons were picked back up by the fierce wind and slung through the air like saucers, crashing through walls and windows. Barrels of wheat, flour, grain, and even pickles rolled along the ground, striking anything in their paths, as the tornado suck everything toward itself with its powerful vacuum. The storm's powerful force destroyed anything it hit as it passed through Indianapolis.

Although Richard had heard about the tornados in the Midwest, he couldn't fathom the fact that people lived with them as a part of their daily lives. The twister's roaring finally ceased, and the conductor assured them it was okay to venture back outside. To their amazement, the tornado seemed to have selected which buildings to destroy and which ones to spare, as if it had some kind of twisted conscience of its own. Johnnie was amazed at what he saw and couldn't believe how some of the buildings had been destroyed by the wild storm. To him, it looked as though they had been demolished by exploding powder kegs or dynamite. Little Johnnie was stunned by how even some of the trees, as big as they were, looked like they were just mere weeds yanked up from a garden and strewn around the ravaged town.

Other people were roaming around, bewildered and crying, as they surveyed the damage and searched for their belongings. Others who hadn't suffered any loss helped the unfortunate victims through their ordeal. Even the DuFours helped others while they waited for the railroad company's storm damage report about the railroad tracks to come back.

While helping others, Pamela stumbled upon a horse that hadn't survived the twister and was partially buried under debris. Johnnie came over to see what his mother had found, but she was reluctant to let Johnnie see the dead horse and covered his eyes.

Richard spoke softly to his wife. "My dear, we must allow our son to see for himself how life can be taken from us in an instant."

"I know you're right, Richard," Pamela whispered. "I know you're right."

Johnnie's eyes grew wide, and he covered his mouth because he was shocked to see the horse. He sighed in sadness for the animal, then turned around and hugged his mother. Word was getting around town that no one had been killed by the tornado, but several injuries were reported, with a broken leg being among the worst.

The train station had been spared, but the train was delayed until the next morning because of debris laying on the tracks. The DuFours would have to wait until then to board and leave for the next town. The following day, Richard, Pamela, and Johnnie boarded the train once again. The family sat quietly, still stunned by what they had experienced. The DuFours waited for the whistle to blow and for the big wheels to turn and take them to perhaps yet another adventure.

While they traveled down the tracks, Pamela said to Richard, "As much as we know about how mechanical things work, we know very little about the weather we live in."

"Oh, how I just hate to leave those poor people behind to fend for themselves!" Pamela said with a quivering voice.

"I know, my dear. Now they have to try to rebuild their lives all over again," Richard said sadly.

As Richard reflected on the tornado, he realized what those odd-looking fan objects were. They were crude tornado-warning systems to alert the people of the general location of a twister.

The next stop was Chicago, Illinois. As the train drew near the city that evening, the full moon was shining bright and high. Johnnie spotted the moon's reflection on Lake Michigan.

"Wow! Is that the ocean, Poppa?"

Richard laughed. "No, son. That's one of the Great Lakes called Lake Michigan," he said. "But it's so big, it might as well be an ocean. The difference between the lakes and the ocean is that the Great Lakes are bodies of fresh water instead of salt water."

Pamela told Richard and Johnnie some of the stories her father had told her about ships getting caught up in bad storms out in the open water, and sinking. The pair listened intently as Pamela described some of nature's fury that can occur out on the lakes. As Pamela neared the end of her stories, Chicago's lights could be seen from the train. The family planned to once again look for a place to eat dinner and find a place to stay overnight so they could leave bright and early the next morning. The train slowed to a stop at one of the city's train stations, but Richard decided they would go on to the next station to get off for the evening.

As the train drew near to the next station, its big wheels slowed to a stop, and the DuFour family got off carrying their luggage and went into town to look for lodging. This city hustled and bustled with its carriage traffic going to and fro for evening activities. The DuFours also noticed the vast number of wooden walkways that were meant to keep people's shoes and clothing from getting muddy when it rained.

That year, the city had received very little rain. The ground was parched, and the wooden buildings were very dry. Richard and his family found a hotel to stay in for the night. After they had dropped off the luggage, the DuFours set off to dine somewhere. When they found a place nearby, little Johnnie looked up to the sky to see if they were going to be interrupted by another tornado. After he was convinced all was clear, the DuFours sat down and had an enjoyable meal together.

After their meal, the DuFours found a nearby theater and attended an opera, which was Johnnie's first. The boy was taken aback at how the singers could sing so loudly and clearly. After the show, the DuFours discussed the program as they headed back to the hotel for a good night's sleep.

During the night, Johnnie had a dream he and his family wound up living in South Dakota for good. Johnnie dreamed that his father was in charge of the big nitroglycerine plant in Creek Canyon. He also dreamed that his family owned a cattle ranch like his great-uncle's in Texas. In Johnnie's dream, the family and their hired hands worked on the ranch, and he spent his free time running wildly through the wide-open, golden wheat fields. Johnnie envisioned his mother carrying a picnic basket and blanket while walking with him and his father to a large, solitary tree that stood in the middle of the wheat field against the big, open, blue sky. There, Johnnie's family enjoyed a homemade lunch under the shelter of the big tree.

Johnnie also dreamed about going to school in a small church building used for schooling during the week. The church building had a bell tower on top of it. Every day, the schoolteacher would ring the bell in the morning when school was about to begin and for recess times. He dreamed that one day, someone started to ring the bell on a Saturday, and he didn't understand why. Johnnie watched the bell ring and ring and ring. Suddenly, he woke out of his dream.

While Johnnie lay there, he heard the ringing again! Startled, Johnnie knew he wasn't dreaming anymore. The ringing grew louder and louder, and soon he heard galloping horse hooves racing up the street to where he and his family were lodging. Johnnie heard men yelling out, "Yah! Yah! Yah!" as the sound of a horse-drawn carriage with a clanging bell sped by his window in the street below. While Johnnie wondered what was going on outside, he heard the same thing again as another horse-drawn carriage sped by!

When Johnnie heard a bell clanging in the distance a third time a couple minutes later, he woke his mother and father.

"Momma, Poppa! Wake up! Please wake up! There's something going on outside!!"

Richard and Pamela jumped out of bed and rushed over to the window to see what was happening. As a third carriage rushed by the hotel, Richard noticed it was a horse-drawn fire wagon.

"Humph!" Richard said. "There must be a fire somewhere!"

While the DuFours watched a fourth wagon rush by, they heard yelling coming from the hotel's hallways. The bellhop was running up and down the halls frantically shouting, "Fire! Fire! Fire!" to awaken the sleeping patrons. Richard dashed out into the hallway and stopped the man to ask if the hotel was on fire.

"No! No! The whole city is on fire!" the bellhop yelled.

Richard summoned his family, and they ran outside to assess the situation. The DuFours were shocked to see the dark skies of the night lit up in bright red-orange. They could see many of the city's buildings engulfed in flames as the huge fire raged out of control. At first, Richard thought the city might have been under enemy attack. Just about everywhere they looked, multiple fires were consuming building after building, surrounding them like an arena.

Richard stopped a young man in the street. "Young fellow, has a battle broken out somewhere?" Richard asked.

"I don't know!" the lad said. "I don't know what's going on."

The DuFour family ran back into the hotel to gather their belongings and joined the thousands of people evacuating the city. People with carriages and hauling wagons emptied their cargo to make room for whomever they could pick up as they fled the burning city.

Richard, Pamela, and Johnnie looked on as the firemen tried to control the flames by hand pumping water out of the fire tanker to try to douse the flames. The water spurted out of the hoses, but it was no match for the ever-increasing heat and flames. The fire companies had to retreat from the fires before they themselves were consumed. Other firemen hooked up hoses to the city's fire hydrants and tried to extinguish the flames. After a while, this effort, too, proved to be ineffective against the swift-moving flames.

Almost all the people of Chicago were yelling and crying as they watched their beloved city go up in flames. It took two days for the fires to die down with the aid of some welcomed rain. The rainfall and the firefighters' efforts saved only a portion of the city. The newspapers reported that many people had died, and it was the worst disaster America had seen up until that time. During the day, all that could be seen were buildings collapsing while they were being consumed. At night, the flames could be seen for miles around, as they seemed to lick the darkened sky. After the fire was mostly out, the city lay in ashes, and smoke from still-smoldering timbers choked the air. The DuFour family wandered around with tear and ash-streaked faces, seeing if they could be of any assistance.

While walking around, Johnnie discovered one of death's victims. This time, it wasn't a horse. It was a young woman who had tried desperately to save her child from the fire, and both were huddled together, dead and charred by the flames. This grim discovery was too much for Johnnie to handle on his own, and both he and his mother wept bitterly in each other's arms.

Along with many other evacuees, Richard and his family stayed in tents provided by the Army. As the days dragged on, the DuFours did all they could to help others in the city. Pamela stayed behind to comfort her son, and the two of them helped other women prepare meals in the open fields. In the evenings, Pamela read the Bible to Johnnie to comfort him. On the eighth day after their arrival, some of the railroad systems were in operation again. The DuFours now had the opportunity to continue on their way.

That tragedy later became known as "The Great Chicago Fire of 1871." Much to the surprise of the nation, a cow owned by a woman named Mrs. O'Leary was blamed for starting the fire. In a mishap, the cow kicked over a lantern that ignited some straw in a barn. The flames quickly consumed the dried-out straw and other surrounding buildings.

To continue their journey, the DuFours had to go to another part of town to catch the next train to Minneapolis, Minnesota. More than a week after the fires subsided, Richard and his family left behind yet another devastated city. While on the train, Richard and his family were still in shock by their tragic experience, and this time, it made history. All Johnnie kept thinking about was how such a tragic event could ever happen by the mishap of one lousy cow!

"Why did the fire spread so fast, Poppa?" Johnnie asked.

"Well, son, apparently the city received very little rain over the summer, making everything so dry that it ignited like a tinderbox," Richard said.

"There must be a better way to prevent such a tragedy! Don't you think, Richard?" Pamela asked.

"If only they had better firefighting equipment to battle such blazes," Richard mumbled over and over again.

Johnnie then said to his father, "Maybe one day they'll make fire wagons using those gasoline engines that can pump more water!"

Richard and Pamela were astonished at their son's reasoning. It was as if he were envisioning a good use for the newly invented internal combustion engine. Richard put his arm around his son's shoulders and said, "You may be right, my son. You may be right."

The next stop on the way to Minneapolis was Madison, Wisconsin. There, the family got off the train to relax a bit and to eat lunch. From Madison, Pamela wired both her father and brother to tell them of the horrific events she and her family had experienced. Pamela also let her family know they were okay, even though the trip had been delayed for well over a week. The DuFours walked the streets as they waited for the train to be greased, oiled, and reloaded with coal and water. This time, however, the DuFours didn't do too much in town because they were still exhausted from everything that had happened since the tornado in Indianapolis. The three weary Easterners made their way back to the train station to get back on the train to head to Minneapolis for the night.

The train chugged away from the station at Madison, and Johnnie fell asleep across his parents' laps, despite the bumping and bouncing of the train cars. When they finally arrived at Minneapolis, Johnnie's parents woke him up. Richard and Pamela found an inn to sleep at and had a quick meal in the dining area. As the DuFours made their way up the stairs to their room, Johnnie hoped he wouldn't hear any more bells in his dreams—or anywhere else, for that matter!

The next day, Richard and his family boarded the train once again to head west. They finally saw the sign for South Dakota that afternoon. The three of them cheered; they were closing in on their final destination. The first stop in South Dakota was Sioux Falls. Richard and his family got off there as they had been doing all along to stretch their legs and observe their surroundings before getting back on the train. The DuFours were eager to press onward to their final stop in Rapid City, South Dakota.

The rest of the trip went well, and even though the trip to Rapid City was a long one, the DuFours were very relieved to get there late in the evening. The DuFours managed to find a small hotel where they could spend the rest of night before they had to prepare themselves for the ride into Creek Canyon by stagecoach.

Richard, Pamela, and Johnnie had finally made it to their final destination. They only had a little ways to go before the journey would finally be complete. The DuFours were filled with joy, and Pamela wired her family once again to tell them she had made it safe and sound.

CHAPTER FOUR

Creek Canyon

The sun rose early, revealing the bright blue, clear morning sky. The air was cool and dry when the DuFour family sat down in the dining area to sample the hotel's morning meal. To Johnnie's surprise, he spotted blueberry flapjacks on the menu.

"Poppa! Blueberry flapjacks like back home! Can we please have some of these? Can we, Poppa?" an eager Johnnie asked.

"Sure thing, my boy. As long as your mother wants some too," Richard replied.

"Well, of course we can!" Pamela said with a smile.

When the waitress delivered the DuFours breakfast of blueberry flapjacks, bacon, coffee, and orange juice, she struck up a conversation.

"Where are you folks from?" she asked.

"We're from back East," Pamela answered.

"From Saratoga, New York, to be exact," Richard added. "Home of the finest race horses in all the land!"

"And the best blueberry flapjacks too!" Johnnie shouted.

"Shhhh! Keep it down, son; we don't want to wake the others," Richard said.

"I see," the waitress replied. "Why are you folks so far from home?"

Richard sat up straight and wiped off his glasses. "The U.S. government required my expertise in engineering to oversee a big project for a few months. So I agreed to their request as long as I could bring my family along with me."

Johnnie noticed that the waitress was an Indian. "Are you a real Indian, lady?" Johnnie asked.

"Jonathan!" Pamela said with a nervous laugh. "What tribe are you from?" Johnnie asked her. Richard chuckled too. "That's enough, my son."

"No, no, that's alright, my little friend," the waitress replied with a smile. "I'm of the Yankton tribe—a part of the Sioux."

The DuFours nodded with interest.

"Are you folks staying here in Rapid City?" the waitress asked.

"No, ma'am," Richard answered. "My business takes me to Creek Canyon where they are building the largest nitroglycerine plant in the country to make dynamite for the copper mines."

At this news, the young Yankton waitress became very silent, and the smile dropped from her face. She glanced at their plates of food and then moved swiftly away. The DuFours looked at one another in confusion, wondering why the sudden change in the waitress's friendliness. When they were done eating, Richard said good-bye to the young lady after he had paid for the meal, but she only acknowledged him with a slight nod.

Richard and his family asked around town for the telegram office. When they found it, Richard wired a message to a government official on the other side of Rapid City telling him of their arrival. Richard got a message back saying the official would meet them at the telegram office in Creek Canyon later that afternoon.

The time had come to catch the stagecoach for the final trip to where the DuFours would be staying. The team of horses came clomping down the dusty street, preceded by the sound of their jangling harnesses. The stagecoach's leaf springs creaked and squeaked as it drew near the area where Richard and his family were waiting. The DuFours' excitement continued to build as they helped the driver load their luggage on top of the coach.

Richard helped his wife into the coach and climbed in after Johnnie, who sat across from his parents, facing them. The DuFours expected others to board the coach with them, but when the driver snapped his reins, the team of horses started to pull the coach ahead, and the DuFours realized they were the only passengers. Soon, they had left Rapid City behind.

The ride toward Creek Canyon was hot and dusty as they traveled down the bumpy road. The stagecoach bounced up and down and back and forth, thrashing the family of three around inside. In the distance, the Black Hills Mountains protruded into the cloudless, blue sky. The foliage displayed some of the most spectacular colors the DuFour family had ever seen. They were quiet as they observed their surroundings—so different from what they were used to. They even spotted different kinds of wildlife and various species of birds in the fields.

After everything the DuFours had been through, however, the Yankton waitress's sudden mood change stuck in their minds. Pamela turned to Richard. "Why do you suppose that Yankton girl grew so quiet after you told her your business, Richard?"

"I really don't know, my darling. But I have the feeling it had something to do with Creek Canyon," Richard said.

"What could it be about Creek Canyon?" Pamela asked. "Yeah, Poppa, what *could* it be?" Johnnie added.

Richard thought for a few moments. "I really don't know, but I'm certain we'll find out soon enough."

As the DuFours reflected on the conversation with the Indian girl, they had no idea what may have caused the young girl's sudden discomfort.

$$* \quad * \quad * \quad *$$

Meanwhile, an old Yankton medicine man was walking along the same road returning from his long vision quest. As the peaceful gentleman walked, he chanted to the spirits, waving his arms toward the sky and to God, whom the Yankton called "Creator." As the old man was chanting prayers, four cowboys rode toward him in a cloud of dust. The elderly man had nowhere to hide out in the open flat lands. The men on horseback called out, "Whoa," as they pulled their horses to a stop. The medicine man stopped walking and stood peacefully smiling at the men sitting on their horses.

One of the cowboys asked him, "Where are you going there, old boy?"

"I am on vision quest, and I am returning back to my people," the old man said.

"Is that so?" another man said.

"What if we don't want you in these parts?" another cowboy asked.

"Please, let me be on my way," the Yankton man pleaded.

"We'll decide whether you go or not, old man!" the first cowboy growled.

The four cowboys dismounted and circled the elderly man. "Well, well, well, what do we have here?" one of the four asked.

"Looks like an intruder to me, boys!" another said.

In an instant, one of the cowboys pushed the old man to the ground and yelled at him. "We don't take kindly to your type, old man!"

As the old man pleaded with the cowboys to stop, they started kicking him. The four of them kicked him in the ribs, the back, and the stomach. The cowboys even kicked the old Indian in the head. Suddenly, one of the cowboys yelled, "Hey! Someone's coming!" The four horsemen abruptly stopped kicking the medicine man.

*   *   *   *

In the stagecoach, the DuFours were enjoying a peaceful ride to the small mining town. After a few minutes, the stagecoach slowed, and the three Easterners peered out the window to see what was going on.

"Look!" Pamela gasped. "Up ahead, on my side!"

The group of men was standing in a circle around the old man, staring at the stagecoach as it approached. As the coach drew near the scene, Richard squinted into the sun and could barley see a man lying facedown in the dirt. The driver slowed the horses to a walk.

"You men need any help?" the driver asked.

"You best just keep right on a-going there, mister!" one of the men yelled back.

With a snap of the reins, the nervous driver commanded the horses to pick up speed again.

"Richard, I am certain I saw a man lying in the dirt!" Pamela said. "It looked like those other men standing around him were tormenting him!"

"Stop this coach!" Richard called out to the driver.

"Why do you want to do that?" the driver asked.

"Just stop this coach this instant!" Richard shot back.

Pamela and Johnnie were shocked at how Richard yelled at the driver and were frightened by his command. The coach stopped.

"Now, you two stay put," he told Pamela and Johnnie.

"But, Poppa …" Johnnie said nervously.

Richard put his finger to his mouth. "Shhhh! Not another word, Johnnie."

Richard slowly opened the door of the coach while the cowboys watched him suspiciously.

Richard climbed up to where the luggage was stowed and opened the box with the guns in it. He then pulled out a gun belt with two holsters and removed the two pistols that were in the box. Richard told the driver to wait right there while he slipped the bullets into the guns' chambers. Richard also asked the driver for a water canteen.

"Richard, please!" Pamela said with a worried look on her face.

Johnnie sat there silently as his father had instructed, but he was just as frightened as his mother. Richard slung the canteen's strap over his shoulder and put on the gun belt with the pistols in their holsters. Richard noticed the cowboys' guns were in their holsters with the holding straps undone and ready to be drawn.

"You folks doing this gentleman any harm?" Richard asked as he approached the group.

"Why? You some kind of Injun lover or sumptin', mister?" one of the cowboys answered.

"I care for the well-being of all people," Richard shot back.

"Look here, mister. You'd better mind your own business if you know what's good for ya!" another cowboy said.

"I can't do that," Richard said.

"Then I guess you'll have ta suffer the consequences, won't ya?" a third cowboy said.

The four cowboys drew their weapons. Being a good marksman, Richard drew his two pistols and instantly shot off the cowboys' hats. The cowboys crouched in surprise at Richard's shooting skills.

At the sound of gunfire, Pamela and Johnnie grabbed a hold of each other and ducked down in the stagecoach. Pamela screamed, "Dear God, help us!" The driver ducked behind the luggage, and the horses jumped at the sudden cracking of gunfire and almost took off. The cowboys slowly got up off the ground.

"I may be wearing a pair of spectacles, but I know where I'm shooting!" Richard yelled.

The four cowboys assumed Richard was a traveling gunfighter and didn't want to take their chances on getting shot. Richard ordered the horsemen to leave the old Yankton man where he lay and go on their way. The four dusty men mounted their horses, and with a quick, loud "Yah!" they galloped away in a cloud of dust. Richard walked back to the stagecoach.

"I'm okay, everybody! Just a little shook up, that's all." Richard assured his family. "Don't worry. Nobody got hurt."

"Please keep the coach still," Richard instructed the driver.

Richard walked over and knelt beside the man to examine his injuries, which looked severe. Richard gently lifted the Yankton man's head to try to give him some water from the canteen. The old man knew Richard was trying to help him and took a few sips. The old Indian chanted something very softly in the Yankton language to Richard, but Richard didn't understand what he said.

"Hang in there, old fellow, hang in there," Richard repeated as he tried to comfort the man.

By way of gratitude, the old man looked at Richard and chanted a different chant. Richard wiped some of the blood off of the Indian's forehead. The spiritual man slowly opened up a little leather bag he had around his neck and put his finger in the bag. It contained a blackish powder used for face painting. The old man slowly reached up to Richard's forehead and drew a symbol while chanting what seemed to be a blessing. Richard let the feeble Yankton continue, because he thought that whatever the man was doing must have been important to the old fellow. After that, the old man drank again from the canteen and slowly relaxed, closing his eyes.

When the old man closed his eyes, a loud screeching sound filled the air. Startled, Richard looked up to the sky and saw a magnificent male American bald eagle flying overhead. The eagle shrieked again, and this time, the sound seemed to pierce Richard's heart. The old Yankton remained still with a smile on his face as the eagle above them screeched, the eerie sound echoing off the mountains.

Pamela and Johnnie weren't watching what was going on because they were still taking cover in the stagecoach. While Richard was looking down on the injured man, a group of shadows appeared around them. Richard slowly turned around, figuring the cowboys had returned. He was surprised to see a group of Yankton warriors pointing spears at him! Not knowing the language, Richard slowly held up his hands.

Trembling, he said to them, "He needs help, he needs help!"

As the warriors approached Richard and the old man with their spears still drawn, the leader of the group, Fighting Bear, noticed the symbol on Richard's forehead.

"He has been blessed! He has been blessed!" Fighting Bear exclaimed to the others in their language.

Pamela, Johnnie, and the driver heard Fighting Bear and were surprised and frightened at what they saw. They could only hold their breaths and hope everything would turn out okay.

"You not from here?" Fighting Bear asked in crude English to Richard.

Richard was stunned, yet relieved, to hear the warrior speak some English.

"No, my family and I are from the East. We saw some men doing harm to this old man and stopped to help."

"We see Bright Moon has blessed you," Fighting Bear said, nodding toward the old man.

Richard explained as best he could that the old man was very weak and needed help. The other warriors dismounted their horses and erected a travois, a bed made up of two wooden poles and woven grass for the center. The warriors suspended one end of the travois from the rear of a horse while the other end dragged on the ground. The Yankton hunters planned to use this device to transport the injured man back to the village.

"He is in our hands now," Fighting Bear said.

The warriors wrapped the old man in a blanket to shield him from the blazing sun.

"I pray that he gets well," Richard said.

The warriors nodded to Richard to acknowledge his help and left with the old man.

Back at the coach, Pamela and Johnnie looked to Richard for answers. As the coach started on its way to Creek Canyon, Richard told his family what the warriors said. Pamela and Johnnie were relieved nobody was hurt or killed.

"What's that on your head, Poppa?" Johnnie asked.

"I don't know, Jonathan." Richard answered.

"Darling, may I please see your little mirror?" Richard asked his wife.

The symbol on Richard's forehead was shaped like an eye with a squiggly mark drawn through it. Richard didn't know what the symbol meant, but he knew that it had saved his and perhaps his family's lives. Richard drew the symbol on a piece of paper to remember it before wiping it off his forehead.

After being a couple of weeks late, the DuFours finally arrived at Creek Canyon, and they cheered as they rolled into town. The family had to stop at the telegram office to meet a government official who was already waiting for them.

Richard walked into the office with his papers to prove his identity. The government official would show the DuFours where they were going to live for the next few months.

"I'm sorry we have arrived so late," Richard said to the government official.

"We were met with much difficulty on our journey."

"You mean the fire in Chicago?" the government man asked.

"Why yes!" Richard answered in surprise.

"That news reached all around the country," the official said. "It was the biggest fire this country has ever seen!"

"We were also struck by a tornado in Indianapolis," Richard said.

"So, I see," the government man said." Unfortunately, those things happen quite frequently in that part of the country this time of year."

While waiting for Richard and the government official, Pamela and Johnnie noticed most of the townspeople were men dressed in very crude clothing. They also noticed how most of the passing people took note of the strangers in town and couldn't keep their eyes off of the Easterners. The town consisted of buildings constructed mostly of wide vertical clapboards with flat tin roofs. Only a few of the structures were constructed of brick or stone.

"Why are there hardly any women or children here, Poppa?" Johnnie asked when Richard returned to the stagecoach.

"Well, son, this kind of town is called a mining town, and it's usually meant for working men only," Richard answered. "Most men here are temporarily away from home like us but couldn't bring their families with them."

The government official climbed aboard the stagecoach with the driver to give directions to get to the DuFours' new homestead.

"Are you folks ready?' the government man called out to the DuFours. "Yes, sir, we're ready!" Richard, Pamela, and Johnnie called back.

The family of three wore big smiles as the stagecoach rolled down the wide, dusty street toward their new home. The DuFours arrived at the house and the small barn the government had provided them for their stay. The house was not quite what the DuFours had expected. It was a one-story structure made up of the same type of clapboarding and tin roofing as the buildings in town. The barn was only large enough to house two horses in the lower part with a small hayloft above.

The homestead, however, was outside of town and had an open field with some large trees in the center like in the dream Johnnie had in Chicago. The family unloaded their luggage with the coachman and the government official's help. Before the coach left, the government man gave Richard a map to the nitroglycerine plant. On the map, Richard saw the road leading to the hydro dam that supplied the plant's waterpower. The government official told Richard he was to report to the plant's office on Monday, giving Richard the weekend to settle into his family's temporary home.

Richard, Pamela, and Johnnie entered their new house through the kitchen and noticed it was stocked with western-style furnishings and two woodstoves. One stove would heat one end of the house; the other was for cooking and heating the other end of the house. The home had no real dining room, but the kitchen area was large enough for a long table made up of two wide boards. The crude kitchen also had some chairs so the DuFours could eat their meals fairly comfortably. The bedrooms were two basic rooms, and each had a rope bed with a freestanding wooden wardrobe. The house wasn't what the DuFours were used to back East, but it would be their home for the time being.

When evening arrived, Pamela took some time to get used to working the kitchen stove. A pile of logs of all sizes sat in the wood room that was attached to the house. Pamela found some kindling and started a fire in the cooking stove. She didn't have any meat to cook that night; the food the government had supplied was either canned in jars or pickled. Pamela also found some grain, cornmeal, and flour to bake with. The DuFours knew they would spend the next day shopping in town for more supplies.

That night they ate heated vegetables and pickled cucumbers and drank water for dinner. This was not anything like the restaurants the DuFours had dined in on their way to South Dakota. After their meal, the tired DuFours turned in for the night.

Saturday morning arrived with bright, cool sunshine and a slight breeze rustling through the trees. The birds in the area were of a different species and sang different morning songs than those back East. Pamela rose earlier than the rest of her family to see what she could make for breakfast. She found ingredients to make some grits that somewhat resembled the flapjacks of home. Before they ate, the DuFours gave thanks to God for protecting them and keeping them on their journey.

After they finished breakfast, little Johnnie went outside to observe the local wildlife. After a few minutes, Richard noticed his son staring at a cluster of scrub brush and wondered what Johnnie was looking at. A little spotted sandpiper bird ran out from under one of the small bushes. Johnnie stood motionless so he wouldn't scare the bird away. The sandpiper looked up at him and made a *peet-tweet-tweet* sound as if saying hello. Johnnie took a liking to the cute little bird. From that time on, the spotted sandpiper was Johnnie's favorite little pet, and he fed it often in the morning before doing his daily chores.

Richard hitched the two horses to an open wagon provided by the government, and the DuFours headed for town to shop for supplies. Creek Canyon wasn't exactly bustling with action, as were the other cities they'd been in. Others rode in crude horse-drawn carts and wagons, but most of the people were on foot carrying a sack of some sort. Some people were at the small assay office to have their silver and gold findings weighed after they had panned them out of the nearby streams. Other locals were buying tools for their personal use.

The DuFours found their way around the town and soon learned where to go to purchase the items they needed. They even found a small slaughterhouse to get a supply of meat. One of the storekeepers told them about a small farm just outside of town where they could buy their chickens and eggs. Instead of raising cows for milk, the area farmers raised goats for milk and beef cattle for meat. The DuFours would have to learn to drink the goat's milk for their breakfast needs.

As the day wore on, Pamela noticed a few shops that sold clothing and shoes.

"Dear, is it alright if Johnnie and I take a look in some of these shops?" she asked Richard.

"Why sure, my love. Take your time," Richard replied. "I'm going to go into this saloon to ask if there are any places to worship around here."

The saloons in the little town were plentiful. Everywhere the DuFours went, sounds of laughter, shouting, and piano music spilled from their open doors and windows. The saloon near the clothing shop, however, seemed to be fairly quiet.

Richard slowly walked through the swinging doors, and all the patrons took note of him being a stranger in town. Some of the men were playing cards, while others were talking quietly at the bar among themselves. Richard noticed one group of four men sitting at a table glaring at him, but he passed it off to being a new face in town. Richard approached the bar reluctantly because he wasn't a whiskey drinker.

The bartender walked over to him. "What'll it be, stranger?"

Richard motioned with his finger for bartender to draw nearer to his face.

Richard reluctantly asked the man for a sarsaparilla in a low voice.

"A sarsaparilla?" the man asked loudly.

"Why, yes," Richard replied a little louder.

The men at the bar snickered.

"Well, let's see here …" the bartender said sarcastically.

The rough-looking man found a bottle of sarsaparilla. "Here ya go, mister!" he said loudly.

The bartender blew some dust off the bottle in front of the others, which made some of the men laugh even louder.

"One sarsaparilla for the gentleman!" the bartender said with a laugh.

More of the men in the saloon joined in on what they considered to be the day's joke. Richard started to laugh a little himself, figuring he was out of the ordinary and knowing he must look silly in a bar drinking anything other than whiskey. Richard once again motioned for the bartender to come over so he could ask him another question. Smiling, the bartender walked back over to Richard.

"Can I get the man some milk this time?"

The others at the bar laughed again and shook their heads.

"My family and I are new in these parts, and we haven't seen any churches," Richard said nervously. "Do you or any of these folks know of any churches around here?"

"Churches!" a scruffy-bearded man yelled out.

Everyone in the saloon fell silent. The bartender's eyebrows rose, and he yelled out, "Any you boys know of any churches around here?"

"There are lots of churches around here, mister!" one man yelled back from one of the tables.

"Well, where are they?" Richard asked.

"You're standin' in one of them right now!" another man said, chuckling.

The patrons broke out in laughter. "Yeah, and this is our time to worship!" another miner yelled from the bar.

After that, the men laughed and carried on about the saloon being a house of worship. One man even yelled out while holding up a glass of whiskey, "We're taking communion, and this is the Lord's blood!"

On and on the patrons heckled Richard and joked about worshiping. An old miner standing next to Richard spoke up. "Men in these parts worship whiskey and gold, my friend."

"You see, mister, this here is 'Hell Town'," the man continued. "If you wanted to worship God, you and your family will need to travel up to the town of Pringle."

"Thank you for your time," Richard said.

As Richard walked out of the saloon, one of the others yelled out to him, "You sure you don't want to worship the golden calf with us?"

The whole place broke out in laughter that could be heard out in the streets.

Richard met up with his wife and son, who were waiting for him outside the clothing store.

"What's all the commotion about in there?" Pamela asked.

"These folks worship nothing but whiskey and gold around here!" Richard said. "We'll have to travel a good hour or so up to Pringle to go to church, I guess."

"Why is that, Poppa?" Johnnie asked. Before his father could answer, the little boy voiced another question. "How could all these men stay dirty like this?"

"Well, son, some people only think of things of this world and forget all about worshiping God," Pamela said in a sad tone.

"To answer your second question, son, men around here are hardworking folks, and they don't have much money to buy clean clothes," Richard said.

The DuFours boarded their wagon and talked about their new town.

"Well, I did find a store to buy about some clothes, shoes, boots, and hats we could use," Pamela told Richard.

"There's an assay office where miners can weigh gold, silver, and even copper," Richard said. "There's also a bank and the telegram office where you can send your family messages from time to time."

"I didn't see hardly any children around here either, Poppa," Johnnie said. "Well, son, perhaps they were all at home doing some chores," Richard said. While the DuFours were heading home, they noticed a man walking beside a donkey. As they approached, the man slowly pulled his donkey off the road to let the wagon by. Richard slowed the two horses to a stop.

"Good day, mister!" Richard said. "My name is Richard, and my sire name is DuFour."

"Hello to you, too, Richard," the man said. "My name is Daniel, but folks around here call me 'Dan the nature man.'"

Richard then introduced his wife and son to Daniel.

Daniel was a prospector who lived like a nomad, traveling from place to place.

Daniel's donkey carried all of his possessions, which consisted of a small, roll-up tent, blankets, water canteens, and some pots and pans that clanked together as they walked. Daniel was a friendly fellow with long, thick, graying hair and a bushy beard and mustache that hid most of his face. The DuFours invited him over for dinner, and Daniel accepted their offer graciously, eager for a home-cooked meal.

Back at the house, while Pamela was cooking dinner, Richard and Daniel talked about their lifestyles in the barn.

"I attended college in Toronto, Canada, where I obtained a degree in plant engineering," Richard said. "I also went to school in Albany, New York, where I got my chemical degree as well."

"Why shiver me timbers, mister!" Daniel said. "You sure is sumptin' with all that schoolin' and all! Heck, when I was a boy, I barely made it through the fifth grade!"

Daniel was intrigued with Richard's education in chemistry and the fact that the government had asked him personally to travel all that way for assistance.

Richard was amazed at how many men lived in the mountains panning for gold, hoping to strike it rich ever since the gold rush of the 1840s. When Richard told Daniel about his saloon experience, Daniel laughed a little.

"The men in these parts don't want to worship anything above the ground," he said. "They only want to worship what's *in* the ground."

Richard also told the mountain man of the run-in with the cowboys on the road to Creek Canyon. Daniel shook his head and said, "Oooh, boy! These boys around here don't take kindly to Indians."

"So, tell me, old fellow. Why do folks think so harshly about the Indians?" Richard asked.

Daniel shook his head. "The Indians are living in the way of the mining operations from what I hear. Getting in the way of progress, folks say."

Richard was troubled at what he heard and slowly shook his head.

After their discussion, they walked to the house for dinner. For the first time in a long time, Daniel had roasted chicken and canned vegetables. Also for the first time, Johnnie and his parents tried the goat's milk. Daniel loved the milk, but the DuFours found it to have a stronger taste than the cow's milk they were used to. Nonetheless, the DuFours and Daniel drank every drop of the goat's milk as if it were a treat.

"Would you like to stay a bit longer, my friend?" Richard asked Daniel.

"No, no thank you. But much obliged for the meal!" Daniel said.

Daniel told the DuFours he had better get going to his spot up in the hills.

Richard offered Daniel some food to take with him and told the mountain man that he and his donkey were always welcome to come by for food and hay anytime. Daniel put on his old cowboy hat with its folded-up brim, thanked the family kindly, and he and his donkey headed off to the hills. The DuFours sat around the light of an oil lamp for a bit and talked about their new surroundings before turning in for the night.

Sunday morning arrived much like Saturday did, with the birds singing outside and the cool sunshine shining through the windows. The DuFours rose early to eat a breakfast of flapjacks, but this time, they were laced with raspberries instead of blueberries. The raspberries were more plentiful in the area, and the DuFours enjoyed them wholeheartedly. After the morning meal, the three left for Pringle to locate a church.

The ride was long and harsh in the stiff wagon, but nonetheless, the family made it safe and sound. The DuFours found a place to worship but had missed the morning Sunday school class by arriving later than they had anticipated. The family attended the noontime worship service, however, and enjoyed the sermon about the love of money being the root of all evil. Richard thought the sermon would be very appropriate for the townspeople of Creek Canyon to hear.

After the services, Richard introduced his family to the preacher, elders, and some of the congregational members. Richard, Pamela, and Johnnie were pleased with the church and planned to attend the church in Pringle, even though the ride to and from the quaint little town was long and rough. The DuFours were satisfied about the progress they were making.

CHAPTER FIVE

The Nitroglycerine Plant

Monday morning rolled in, bringing the start of new routines for everyone. Johnnie had been out of school for nearly two months, so he had to be enrolled at the school in Creek Canyon. But the family had a lot to do around the farmhouse before they could enroll him. They had chores, cleaning, and tending to the horses in the small barn. Richard and Pamela decided to keep Johnnie home for another week until they were well settled in. Pamela tackled the task of rearranging the furnishings to the family's liking so they could really feel like the house was their home.

Richard was to start his new job overseeing the operations at the nitroglycerine plant. He was responsible for helping other engineers with the processes of producing ingredients for dynamite. Richard's morning consisted of washing up, eating a good breakfast, putting on proper attire for the day, and organizing his paperwork for the job. Richard kissed his family good-bye and hitched up a horse and buggy to head off to the plant.

Richard had the first-day jitters and tried to ease his mind by observing his surroundings as he rode into town. He took note of the different varieties of trees, shrubbery, and other vegetation that grew in the area. He also observed the wildlife and different species of birds to take his mind off the day's upcoming business. As he arrived in town, Richard again noticed little activity and hardly a woman or child to be seen. The plant was located just outside of town, heading north into the narrow canyon.

Richard arrived at the planning office of the Creek Canyon Chemical Company, unhitched his buggy, and led his horse into the plant's stable.

He gathered up his belongings and entered the planning room for the new operations, where he met with a building engineer.

"Hello, my name is Richard DuFour, and I'm the chemical engineer from Saratoga, New York," Richard said.

"My name is Michael Gordon, and I'm from Sacramento, California," the building engineer said.

The two men shook hands and met with the contractors who would install the steam-powered circulation system. The system was designed to direct chemicals, including liquid nitroglycerine, to different areas of the plant. Everyone sat down at a large drafting table, and the two engineers unrolled their blueprints and clamped down the edges to hold them flat.

The engineers were interested to view each other's plans. Each plan was like the piece to a giant puzzle, ready to be fitted together to form an operating system. Richard had the blueprints of how the chemicals needed to flow and mix within the plant's pipelines. He also had blueprints of the steam-powered furnace to heat water into steam and direct the steam into a large, twenty-foot-high accumulator tank. After it was up to pressure, hand-operated valves would direct the steam through the various pipelines. The contractors also had plans on how the separate iron pieces of the pipelines and the accumulator tank would be riveted together on-site within the facility. Michael had the blueprints of the plant's structure itself. The prints contained important information on how the major support beams would hold up the factory's massive roof.

Lunchtime came upon the men very quickly, and they went to a small tavern nearby for their break. The excited engineers continued to discuss business over lunch. After the break, they walked around the almost completed building. Richard and the others observed the plant's structure and got a firsthand look at where the pipes would be hung from the rafters. The men also inspected the room where the location of the main furnace was to be.

Richard was having a field day. Not only was he looking at the other engineers' interesting sketches, but he was also viewing the structure of what was to be the largest chemical plant in the world! He was fascinated by how the large steel beams were fastened together, and also by the way the large wooden ductwork was laid out to house the pipelines. The plant itself spread out over an area of about ten acres, and some sections of it towered seven stories high. The plant's walls were made up of brick supplied by several brickyards from surrounding towns. The roof was overlaid with heavy tin that sloped slightly in different directions.

It seemed to Richard that many of the workers on the site worked as carpenters and bricklayers. Richard figured this was probably where most of the townspeople were employed because there didn't seem to be many other businesses except for the stores and saloons.

Richard made it a point to meet the builders and introduce himself. "Good day, my name is Richard DuFour, and I'm the chemical engineer," Richard said to them. "How are you fellows doing today?"

Some of the workers were open to his politeness, while others didn't want to be bothered by him. A certain group of bricklayers, however, just stared at him as Richard tried to talk to them. He thought he recognized the group from somewhere else and tried to think of where he had seen them. Then Richard remembered the group of four men at the saloon who had just sat there and stared at him, in much the same way these men were doing now. Richard figured these men might have felt threatened by strangers coming into town to take away jobs.

Richard and the other engineers moved on to speak to the supervisors about the project. After some time, they all went back to the office and to the drafting tables. They poured themselves some water and began to discuss their observations from the plant tour. The engineers spent the rest of the day planning how the plant project would come together, step by step, in the next few months.

After work, Richard stopped by the telegram office to wire Pamela's message to her parents in which she told them about their weekend. He told his in-laws that things were going particularly well so far. After wiring Pamela's parents, Richard wired his own family in Canada about the trip and his new responsibilities in South Dakota. Even though Richard didn't keep in contact with his family very often, he was still close with them. Richard's parents would wire him from time to time to keep him informed of things back home in Canada. By now, Richard had gotten to know the telegram operator pretty well and they took a liking to each other.

Richard went home with high sprits, eager to tell his family about the first day of his new job. A trip to the hydro dam was planned for the next day because it was going to be the major power source for the new plant.

Some of the water power would run some of the grinding rooms where substances such as gunpowder would be made. Richard arrived home to the open arms of his wife and son.

"Well, my dear, how did your day go?" Pamela asked with a big smile. "Oh, fine, just fine," Richard replied.

"Can I go see the plant too, Poppa?" Johnnie asked eagerly.

"Well, son, perhaps after it's all built and finished and in full operation, I'll give you both the grand tour!" Richard said.

"Oh boy! That'll be swell!" Johnnie shouted.

When the DuFours sat down to eat dinner, Richard gave thanks to the Lord and shared more events of his day. That evening, the DuFours relaxed in the living room, which had an open fireplace that could be used on chilly summer nights. When Richard and Pamela went to bed that night, he told her that he would spend the next day viewing the hydro dam's blueprints and traveling up to the dam itself.

"I'm concerned about those blueprints, Pamela," Richard said. "You know I haven't looked at them since we left your brother's home."

Richard had vowed not to open the diagrams until he arrived in Creek Canyon. He had kept his vow, but tomorrow he would have to unroll the drawings so the other men could see them before the tour to the dam.

"I know you're concerned, Richard," Pamela said. "But you know you have to do your duty and pray nothing happens."

"I know you're right, my love," Richard replied. "I just hope that spell doesn't return to me."

Richard and Pamela drifted off to sleep and slept soundly.

On Tuesday, the DuFours went through the same routine, with Pamela and Johnnie taking care of the homestead and Richard preparing for work. As he left the house with the hydro dam's drawings in the leather tube, Richard hugged and kissed his family as he had the previous day. This time, there was a sense of nervousness between the husband and wife concerning Richard's experience with the dam's drawings. The only thing Richard's family could do was to hope for the best for him.

Richard left for work in the buggy and arrived at the job site to view the drawings with the other engineers. They all gathered around the drafting tables once again to look at the plans for diverting some of the hydro dam's waterpower to the new facility. Richard slowly opened the top of the leather tube; his heart was racing. The chemical engineer tried not to show any anxiety in front of the others, but it was hard for him to hide his nervousness. The others sensed his reluctance.

"Are you alright, Mr. DuFour?" one engineer asked him. "You look like you're about to take fever."

"All is well, gentlemen. My health is fine," Richard replied.

Richard opened the sketches. While they all examined the drawings, Richard didn't sense the terrible, haunting experience as he had before. Relieved, he took out a handkerchief and wiped beads of sweat off his brow.

"Hot in here!" he said with a laugh.

Richard was relieved that he and the others could discuss the blueprint without any further concerns. After the discussions and planning, the men decided to ride up to the hydro dam's location and have a closer look at the structure.

The hydro dam not only regulated the town's water supply, but it also supplied power to various operations. It had been erected about ten years before the site for the nitro plant was selected, and it had a maze of large, underground iron pipelines. Water traveled through the pipes to power other operations downstream from the reservoir. Planners found it easier to build the nitro facility near the pipelines to turn the water turbines used to run the plant's equipment.

Richard and the others traveled up the ever-narrowing canyon leading through an area where a very high train trestle extended from one side of the canyon to the other. After passing under the trestle, they proceeded up to the dam.

After the men tied up their horses, they began walking around the grinding rooms and met with some of the workers to talk about the work there. Richard decided to walk down to the base of the hydro dam to inspect the structure up close. As he drew closer to the dam's wall, Richard suddenly started to feel the same spell he felt back in New York. The spell worsened this time and grew even more intense as he stood there looking up toward the top of the dam. The chemical engineer started to hear the faint cries and screams as he had before, but this time, the cries grew even louder and clearer. Richard put his hands over his ears and shouted out loud, "No! Not again! No! Not again!"

Richard fell to his knees. "Please stop! Please stop and go away whoever or *whatever* you are!" Richard pleaded.

On top of all the crying, Richard started to see a vision, as if he were dreaming. Richard saw a night where river water flooded the land. He could barely make out objects and people floating in the floodwaters, but he could hear the people's cries again. The whole experience left Richard shaking and curled in a tight ball on the ground.

The spell and vision slowly lifted, and Richard regained enough strength to stand. For a while, he was confused and dismayed about what had just happened to him. While Richard stood there bewildered, the others came down to him.

"Is there anything to report of the dam, Richard?" one of them asked.

Having forgotten his original reason for being down there, Richard rubbed his forehead. "Everything looks rock solid here," he said. "I just need to get out of the hot sun for a bit, gentlemen."

As Richard went to sit in the shade, the other engineers inspected the hydro dam but seemed totally unaffected by it. Richard kept asking himself why it was only he who was overcome by such a spell and not the others. After the others completed the inspection, they headed back down the canyon and called it a day. The engineers made plans to start overseeing the completion of the plant's structure while they filled out orders for the steam line sections to arrive by train. Richard hitched up his horse and buggy without saying much else to anyone and headed home to his family.

When Richard arrived home, he didn't seem to be himself. Pamela picked up on the mood right away.

"It happened again, didn't it?" she asked him.

"Yes, my dear, it indeed did happen again!" Richard said. "The spell didn't come upon me while I was viewing the drawings, but it happened while I was up at the dam itself! This time the spell was so overwhelming, it knocked me off my feet!"

Pamela was very concerned about what had happened to her husband, and tears started to stream down her pretty, white face. Richard wiped her tears away. "I'm sure there's a reason for all of this. We just have to wait and see what it is, my love."

"Let's all take a walk and clear our minds, for it's such a lovely evening," Pamela said.

While the three of them walked and talked in the field, Johnnie told his mother and father about the dream he had had in Chicago right before the fire.

Johnnie's parents were surprised at how closely his dreams matched their new surroundings.

"Perhaps we're both having these visions for a reason," Richard said.

The DuFours sat down under a large tree and watched the sun set. Suddenly, they heard a man yelling, "Hey there!"

It was Daniel whom they had met on their way back from town over the weekend. Daniel walked out into the field and sat down with the DuFours. "I was up visiting with my friends in the mountains," Daniel told the DuFours.

"What kind of people live up there, Daniel?" Johnnie asked.

"I'm a friend of the Yankton people, and I trade furs for food with them," Daniel said.

The DuFours were surprised. It seemed Daniel was the only other person who actually liked the natives in the area.

"As matter of fact, I was at a burial ceremony for one of their elders," Daniel told Richard.

The DuFours exchanged looks.

"Do you think it was the same old feller you helped back on the road?" Daniel asked.

"It could very well be," Richard said with a grave look on his face.

Richard gave Daniel a vivid description of the old Indian and told Daniel that the man's name was Bright Moon. As it turned out, it was the same old man.

Pamela and Johnnie shed some tears for the old gentleman, and Richard just shook his head sadly.

After those initial days in Creek Canyon, the weeks seemed to fly by. The chemical plant was near completion, and now that the parts for the chemical delivery system were on-site, it was time to start assembling them. There was very little need for Richard to revisit the hydro dam, and he avoided doing so as much as possible. Richard oversaw the assembly of the pipelines and the furnace connection to the accumulator tank. Michael oversaw the construction of the wooden ductwork to house the pipes. They also instructed the men as to how to assemble everything else as well.

One day, just before the project was completed, Richard was alone in the planning office, reviewing the blueprints to ensure all was being followed exactly as it should. He heard a knock at the door and said, "You may enter."

The door slowly opened, and four men walked into the office in single file.

"May I help you men with something?" Richard asked politely.

The four men lined up side by side and stood motionless as they stared at Richard. They were part of the group of workers who were laying bricks. Richard also recognized them from the one table in the saloon.

"We don't want you around here no more, mister!" one of the men finally said.

Astonished at what he heard, Richard slowly looked up at them. "I beg your pardon, gentlemen. I mean you no harm. Why do you no longer want me here?"

Another man spoke up. "You caused us enough trouble already!"

"How do you reckon that?" Richard asked.

The men didn't answer Richard. Instead, they slowly brought their cowboy hats from behind their backs and placed them on their heads. The four men slowly withdrew their hands from the fronts of their hats to reveal a bullet hole in each one of them. The men's glares intensified. Richard finally understood that these were the very same four men whose hats he'd shot off out on the road into Creek Canyon. Richard also knew now that these men were responsible for the old Yankton man's death. Without another word, the four of them slowly left the office in single file, just as they had arrived. Richard felt a cold feeling go right through him. He realized he had murderers working under him!

That evening when Richard got home, he and his family climbed up to the top of a nearby cliff to watch the sun set. A very concerned Richard DuFour told his wife and their son about the events of that day while the three of them sat looking toward the bright red-orange sunset. Pamela took Richard by the hand.

"We are living on a prayer out here, Richard," Pamela said with a soft voice. "Please don't worry, my husband. God is watching over us."

Johnnie could do nothing but hug his father around the waist and keep saying, "Everything will be all right, Poppa. Everything will be all right."

"I know it will," Richard said as he embraced his wife and son.

As the days wore on, the delivery system within the nitro plant seemed to go together relatively easily. The furnace was installed and tested in one week, and the accumulator tank was erected and pressure tested the following Monday. On that day, Richard showed the men how the pressure-relief valve worked. The chemical engineer closed off the outgoing steam pipes from the accumulator tank to demonstrate it.

When up to pressure, the relief valve blew open with a loud train-like whistle that could be heard throughout the canyon. Some of the men had to plug their ears, it was so loud. After that, Richard quickly opened up a larger relief valve by turning a steel wheel by hand. As he cranked the steel wheel, the sudden release of steam gushed into the air through a larger pipe, and the pressure soon dropped to the point where the relief valve stopped whistling.

Richard instructed the men that in case of an emergency, the pressure from the accumulator could be released rather quickly by hand before it would explode. It took some time to make sure the workers knew how to operate the facility safely. As the piping was installed, Richard continued to educate the men about how the water flowed in one end of the system and was boiled so it created pressure in the tank. When pressurized, the steam was released through other pipes to drive various steam-powered equipment. Richard also told the workers what chemicals were transported in the other pipes. He explained that the liquid nitroglycerine had to flow at a certain rate because it was very unstable and explosive. Richard stayed on as an engineer consultant to aid the men while they learned how to deal with the new state-of-the-art equipment.

As Richard's family stayed in the area, the townspeople grew colder toward them. Some started to yell obscenities at the DuFours, calling them "Injun lovers." Even worse, some of the townspeople expressed their desire to see the natives and all who favored them dead. Now Richard knew what Daniel meant by the townspeople "not taking a liking to the Indians." Eventually, people bragged right in front of Richard and his family of killing, or helping to kill, the local Yankton people at one time or another.

The angry people would tell stories of how they'd shot and killed Indians, or how they'd hung them, and even dragged some behind horses. Others told stories of burning their villages in the night and killing them that way. There was even one terrible rumor of a massive drowning of the Yankton people. Stories of torture and murder turned the DuFours' stomachs.

The nitroglycerine plant was in full operation, and all the people wanted was for Richard and his family to leave. However, the government wanted Richard to spend more time in Creek Canyon to ensure no tragic accidents would occur because of a lack of experience. Richard agreed to stay.

Richard finally approached the sheriff about the townspeople's attitude toward the Yanktons.

"Sheriff, I'm afraid there's rumor going around town about numerous murders of the Indians," Richard said to the weathered-looking man.

Sheriff Chad Rippford crossed his arms and slowly sat back in his creaky office chair. "Is that so, mister?" the sheriff replied.

"Why, I'm certain of it!" Richard exclaimed.

"I tells you what, there boy. There ain't nuttin' out of the ordinary goin' on around here, so I suggest you keep your mind on your own business," Rippford said. "Besides, aint you fixin to leave soon anyway?"

"But, but …" Richard tried to continue when the sheriff butted in.

"You just pay no mind to the folks around here, and everything will be just dandy!" the sheriff growled.

As more weeks went by, the prejudice grew even worse. The more Richard heard about murders Daniel confirmed as being true, the more he wanted to do something about it.

One Saturday, Richard and his family took a trip back to Rapid City to file a complaint against the slackness of the Creek Canyon Sheriff's Department. Richard also explained to officials in Rapid City about the townspeople's open confessions about murders they claimed to have committed. The officials in Rapid City informed Richard and his family that the judicial system would look into the matter. Not being satisfied with this answer and feeling powerless, the DuFours headed back to Creek Canyon to see to it that this matter was cleared up and to do what they could to prevent anymore harm.

CHAPTER SIX

One Man against One Town

The seasons were changing and autumn was nearing its end, making way for the winter months. Johnnie attended the local school in Creek Canyon, and the simple schoolhouse was nothing like the nice little church building in his dream back in Chicago. Instead, the schoolhouse was a small, dusty building once used as a storage place for wood before the few women and children arrived in Creek Canyon. The school had a small woodstove in the center of its one room with a stove pipe protruding through the schoolhouse's flat roof.

The desks and chairs were old and worn out, much like the cracked chalkboard the teacher wrote on. The handful of students ranged from the first-to the sixth-grade levels. At first, Johnnie enrolled into the fourth grade like he would have done back in Saratoga. After being tested, though, he was already at the sixth-grade level according to the standards in Creek Canyon. Needless to say, Johnnie was disappointed with the low standards of the town's educational system. When Johnnie told his parents about his grade placement, Richard and Pamela, too, were disappointed with the lack of attention directed toward the school.

The DuFours figured Johnnie would catch up to his own level in the spring after they returned to the East. The DuFours hadn't planned on experiencing a typical long South Dakotan winter, but because little was being done about the many murders of Yanktons taking place, they decided to tough it out. Pamela was busy, too, as she used her canning skills to preserve fruits and vegetables in sealed glass jars. The canned food provided some nutrition for the family along with the vegetables and fruits they obtained from the few farms in the area.

Tensions increased as Richard and his family continued their stay at Creek Canyon. Richard's consulting expertise was needed less often now that the employees of the nitro plant could operate the facility effectively. The time came for government officials to inspect the plant and evaluate the entire operation. The men from Washington stayed in Rapid City while they traveled back and forth to inspect various operations of the plant. The government men also inspected the hydro dam that supplied the water for powering the machinery in the facility. As the men carefully inspected the operations, the workers didn't seem to mind being observed while they went about their daily tasks. After a week of observations, a form was submitted to the sheriff stating everything had passed inspection. A copy of the completed form was also submitted to Richard. It was late November, and Richard's duties were complete in Creek Canyon.

Richard wired Washington concerning his stay in South Dakota. He managed to convince the officials of the industrial movement program to keep him on as a plant manager to ensure that the nitro plant would operate smoothly during the harsh winter months. The man who was originally appointed to the position of manager had to take a backseat to Richard and was reduced to a supervisor's position to oversee the boiler rooms. The newly appointed supervisor was disgruntled when he learned that the very man he and the others wanted out of town had bumped his position. Richard tried to explain Washington's reasoning to the men, but they simply did not accept Richard's explanation as a good answer.

Not only did this add to the men's anger toward Richard, it started a rebellion among the plant's workers. The workers congregated at a saloon one evening and decided to keep the plant running as usual. At the same time, the men conspired against Richard. Things were not looking so favorable for Richard at the Creek Canyon Chemical Company! As time went on, not only did Richard feel the alienation from his own employees, Pamela felt the distancing from the townspeople as well.

At times, store clerks would tell Pamela they were out of stock when in fact the store was not out at all. Other times, shops would charge her more money than the original prices. Johnnie also felt the pressure from his peers in school. Although few children attended the school, they formed their own cliques, excluding Johnnie. The teacher tried her best to keep the others from singling Johnnie out, as well as keeping them from totally disregarding him altogether.

One day, Richard and his family were walking by one of the many saloons in town. Three men stood outside the doorway leaning against the wall, each with one foot on the ground and the other heel braced against the wall. Each of the men had a bottle of whiskey in one hand while the other hand was halfway in their pants pockets.

As the DuFours strolled by, one of the drunken men said to Richard, "Hey, mister, ain't you done with what you came here to do?"

"Well, gentlemen, I was called upon to oversee the nitro plant through the winter to make sure operations survive the cold without anything going wrong," Richard said.

"Is that so, mister!" the man yelled back. "We just plain don't want you around here no more, ya hear?"

Richard nudged his wife and son and said in an undertone, "Let's move along. Pay no mind to those men."

As the DuFours continued to walk down the street, one of the three men called out to them, "We're gonna get you yet, *boy*!"

Richard glanced back only once before continuing along with his family. "Poppa, when is all this bad stuff going to end?" Johnnie asked.

"Well, son, unfortunately, I have more business to take care of, and I'm afraid it won't end very soon," Richard replied.

"What kind of business, Poppa?" Johnnie asked.

"Son, I have some personal things to tend to before we can head back home again," he said.

Richard was not speaking of his job at the nitro plant, however. He was referring to the justice that he wanted to see done in town concerning the Indian murders. All Johnnie could think was that he was in for a long, long winter. Richard kept tabs on what he continued to hear around town and discreetly kept in touch with the officials in Rapid City.

One day when Richard went to the telegram office to wire Rapid City more information he had found, the old telegram operator pulled him off to the side. He was a short, skinny man in his mid-sixties with gray hair. The old man always wore a leather visor on his forehead to keep sunlight out of his eyes so he could see the Morse code messages.

"I see how the folks around here are giving you and your family the business," the old man said.

"What do you know about this, my old friend?" Richard asked.

"Well, mister, between you and me, the sheriff and his men are at the bottom of all this," the telegram operator said.

"But *how?*" Richard asked.

"You see, Rippford is in cahoots with all the copper mine owners in these parts, and he has a deal with them to get rid of the Indians!" the operator replied.

"Matter of fact, he got the government to pitch in money to build that there factory you work for."

Richard stepped back a moment and took a deep breath. "The Creek Canyon Chemical Company is the *sheriff's* dealings?"

"Yeeup!" the operator replied.

"But, *why?*" Richard asked in disbelief.

"Miners need land. The land has Indians living on it. The sheriff wants money. He'll do anything for it—even kill!" the operator said.

"How is he getting away with it?" Richard asked.

"Simply put. Rippford is fakin' the papers saying he's movin' the Indians to reservations, and he's even got the townspeople under his iron fist," the operator said. "And I should know. He makes me wire the telegrams to the government."

"Have you ever thought of turning him in?" Richard asked.

"Rippford would skin me alive!" the operator said.

Richard thanked the telegram operator and said little else to him as he wired more information to Rapid City. A couple of weeks later, officials started to arrive in Creek Canyon. The new arrivals started poking around town, asking questions. A suspicious atmosphere formed as the men roamed from place to place.

"Have you seen or heard of any suspicious activities concerning the Yankton people?" one official asked a store clerk.

"No, sir! I ain't seen or heard nuttin' like that around here," the clerk said.

No matter who the officials talked to about the harsh treatment of the Indians, the townspeople's replies were the same. Some of the people suggested that the officials talk to the sheriff instead of questioning them. The officials decided to take the townspeople's advice and walked into the sheriff's office to introduce themselves. "Sheriff?" one of the investigators asked.

"That would be me," Rippford replied. "You boys got business pokin' around here?"

"We were sent here from Rapid City to look into reports concerning mistreatment of the local natives," another official said.

Sheriff Rippford slowly rose up from his creaky old chair and stood in front of the men.

"Is that so," he said.

"Yes, sir," answered the first official.

"Tell you what, boys. If I hear or even find out about any mistreatment to the Indians, I will hold that individual or individuals accountable for their actions," Rippford said.

"Well, Sheriff, we have received an unusual number of reports concerning serious crimes, including murder, against the area's natives," another official added.

The sheriff just glared at them. "Guess you boys didn't hear me very well, did you? If you fellas come up with any proof of what you heard, *then* you come back and see me!" Sheriff Rippford said. "Otherwise, I chalk all this up as hogwash."

The officials, surprised at the sheriff's response, left the office and went about their business in town. Before they left town, however, they stopped back at the sheriff's office.

"Sheriff Rippford," the head official said, "if we receive any more reports about the matter, law enforcement will be sent in from the state to conduct a full investigation."

And with that said, the head official tipped his hat to the sheriff before he and his men rode out of town. After the officials were out of sight, the sheriff and some of his deputies sat down to discuss the events taking place in town.

"We gotta do something about this, boys!" Rippford said. "Word is getting out to the surrounding areas about the way we townspeople deal with these damned Indians."

Scratching their heads, the sheriff's men tried to figure out how the news was spreading all of a sudden. Now every lawman in the state would soon hear about Creek Canyon's actions. As they sat there quietly for a few minutes, one of the deputies said one word that answered all of their questions: "DuFour!"

With the aid of the sheriff and his deputies, the townspeople formed a conspiracy against the DuFour family in an attempt to stop the reports from getting to Rapid City. At first, the workers gave Richard a hard time at the nitro plant, hoping to force him to leave his position, as well as Creek Canyon. Richard called a meeting one morning and told the workers that if there were to be a mutiny in the plant, he would have the government come in and take control of the situation. The townspeople made other attempts to force the DuFours to leave. Women yelled obscenities at Pamela, things like; "You female dog!" or, "You snobby Easterner!"

At school, Johnnie suffered more and more ridicule from his peers, especially in the schoolyard. The children would form a circle and clap their hands to a nursery rhyme they made up to taunt the little boy:

> "Johnnie boy, Johnnie boy, why don't you go home?
> Go back to where you came from, where the buffalo roam.
> We don't want no part of you.
> Johnnie boy, Johnnie boy, shoo, fly, shoo!"

The situation got so bad that little Johnnie had to play by himself or stay behind in the schoolhouse. The scorns persisted against Richard and his family. Then came the threats. Notes were left on their buggy saying, "Leave or else …" at any given time. People shouted from across the street, "We know where you live!" and then quickly looked the other way, making it hard to determine who yelled out.

The threat that concerned Richard the most, though, was one he heard more and more often. The threat was that whatever was done to the Indians would soon be done to them if he and his family didn't leave. Richard eventually sent another report to Rapid City for his family's own protection. While Richard was wiring his reports, the telegram operator kept him informed of what the sheriff was up to.

A day after the report was received in Rapid City, a group of Union officers was sent to Creek Canyon to try to regain control of the situation. The Army men patrolled the streets as if they were guarding prisoners of war. Sheriff Rippford called a meeting with his deputies and the Army's sergeant.

"We want to call a truce between the Union and the townspeople regarding the threats against the DuFours, sir," Rippford said.

"Alright. How about if you call all the townspeople together for a meeting in the town hall at seven o'clock this Saturday?" the sergeant said.

Rippford took out a large gold pocket watch with a silver chain attached to it to observe the time.

"That's a mighty fine timepiece you got there, Sheriff," the sergeant said.

The sheriff quickly slipped the watch back into his shirt pocket and leaned back into his creaky old chair. "Seven o'clock Saturday will do fine. Anything else I can help you boys with?" he asked.

Another officer peered at Rippford's gun belt. "Nickel-plated six-shooters too, I see."

The sergeant tilted his head and looked down at the guns. "Hmm, fancy engravings on them gun barrels, along with pearl handles too," he said. "And both them guns slung in snake-skinned holsters. A bit much for a sheriff's salary, wouldn't you say, Mr. Rippford?"

The sheriff's face turned beet red. "I manage my own wages my way!"

The Army sergeant reached into what appeared to be a mailbag and drew out a document in front of the sheriff. He slowly opened the folded piece of paper and began looking at it. "Says here you're a part of an Indian relocation program—you know, finding places for the Indians to live on reservations."

"Yes, I am," grumbled Rippford.

"Also, according to this, you get a fee for every Indian you place," the sergeant said. "You must be finding a lot of homes for them poor folks, aren't you, Sheriff?"

"Yes, I am!" Rippford shouted.

The Army sergeant said nothing else, tipped his hat to Rippford, and walked out the door with his men following behind.

By the week's end, word got around town about the upcoming meeting at the town hall. By seven o'clock that Saturday evening, the town hall was jam-packed. It seemed as though the town had emptied all of its residents into the meeting hall that very night. The DuFours were escorted to the front row to be protected from any rioting.

The Union officers, armed with loaded rifles, stood on both sides of the pulpit where the sheriff, acting as mayor, was to conduct the meeting. The room soon filled with the low rumblings of the townspeople's voices as they congregated in the hall. All were eager to hear what Sheriff Rippford had to say. The sheriff stepped up to the pulpit and held up his right hand to silence the crowd. As he did so, a series of *shhh, shhh, shhhs* went around the room as the people attempted to silence one another. When the room was silent, the sheriff began to speak.

"Hear ye, hear ye, fellow residents of Creek Canyon. We are all gathered here equally yoked together as brethren in the eyes of God."

The words spoken by the sheriff were surprisingly like those of a preacher. Rippford continued addressing the crowd using phrases from the Bible, such as "loving your fellow man as yourself." As the hypocrite bellowed out about brotherly love for all mankind, Richard was astonished to hear such flowery speech coming from a man who was known for his rough ways of dealing with criminals. Rippford started reciting the various verbal abuses committed by the public against Richard and his family and pretended to condemn them all.

When the crowd grumbled a bit, the sheriff held up his right hand once more to silence them. Rippford asked the crowd, with the Union officers as witnesses, to stop persecuting the DuFours during the remainder of the family's stay. The audience was silent for a moment until one man spoke up.

"Then you tell that Richard DuFour to stop sending out false reports to Rapid City!" he yelled.

The crowd suddenly became noisy again, yelling, "Yeah, yeah, yeah!" in agreement. The sheriff waved both hands in the air.

"Okay, okay, okay," he said. "I'll speak to him privately about that matter."

Just as the sheriff was about to add more sugar to his words, Richard raised a hand to have his say about the whole situation. The sheriff, with a false smirk on his face, gave Richard permission to speak. Richard stood up and turned to face the people. The audience grumbled a bit, but finally quieted enough to hear what he had to say.

"My fellow folks," Richard began. "My family and I suffered much difficulty on our trip westward. We were struck by a tornado in

Indianapolis and also endured a harsh personal experience during the great Chicago fire."

The crowd listened intently while Richard spoke. He explained how the government had selected him because of his expertise in chemicals, to ensure the nitroglycerine plant's safe operation.

"All I wanted to do is help you folks out," Richard said.

"Well, we don't need none of your help no more!" another man shouted.

The crowd grumbled in agreement, giving Richard a moment to think about the very question he had been eager to ask all along.

"Do you have anything else to add, Mr. DuFour?" the sheriff asked.

"Yes," Richard said. "But I don't quite know how to ask my next question."

"Well, Mr. DuFour, no unasked question is a good question," the sheriff falsely encouraged. "Ask, and it shall be given unto you."

Richard paused for a moment. "Why are all you folks so full of hatred against the Indians, anyway?"

All of a sudden, the crowd nearly went into a riot. The townspeople became very noisy, stood up, and yelled all sorts of comments at once. The commotion made it difficult to understand what was being said. The sheriff waved his arms for silence, but the crowd grew even louder. The sheriff pulled out a wooden gavel and slammed it down on the pulpit over and over again to get the crowd's attention. Finally, after about ten minutes or so of shouting, the audience was somewhat under control and seated again. But, by this time, everyone had angry expressions on their faces.

"Well," the sheriff said. "Did you get your answer that time?"

Richard was afraid to say anything at first, but then he spoke up. "Since it was hard to understand anyone, I found it very difficult to get one good answer."

One man jumped out of his seat. "If them damn Injuns would quit telling us this land is theirs, we might be able to get some damned mining done around here and make our money!" he yelled.

The whole crowd jumped up out of their seats once again, waved their hats, and began hooting and hollering. The crowd then started shouting, "Any friend of the Injuns ain't no friend of ours!"

The crowd got so out of hand that they would not even heed the sheriff's hammering on the pulpit. The Union officers had to draw their rifles and cock them while blowing whistles to bring the people back under control. Just as the crowd started to settle down, the four men Richard encountered earlier walked up to the front of the room with their cowboy hats in their hands. The audience grew silent to see what the four men had to say.

The four of them slowly placed their hats on their heads, and just as before, they withdrew their hands from the fronts of their hats, exposing the bullet hole in each one. The crowd gasped.

"This so-called good man of ours tried to shoot us in the head while we were trying to help a poor old Indian man back to his feet!" one of the men said.

The crowd grew wild again as Richard attempted to defend himself and tried to tell them it was all a lie. Some people were so angry that they didn't care if the Union officers fired shots or not. Others were so frightened that they were ready to stampede out of the room. Luckily, no shots were fired, but some of the people yelled to Richard, "I hope you heard us that time, mister!" while others shouted, "Yeah, yeah, yeah!" Only one man in the room sat silently throughout the whole meeting—the telegram operator.

It was nearly midnight when the meeting finally ended, and the crowd returned to their homes without further incident. Richard and his family were exhausted by how the angry crowd felt toward them. All they could do now was hope and pray that all the negativity would soon subside. There was still one problem, though. The murderers still remained at large.

Later that night in the sheriff's office, the Union officers met with the sheriff. "You got yourself a situation here, Sheriff!" one of the men said. "We hope you can clear this matter up before it really gets out of hand!" "Don't you fellas worry," the sheriff said. "I'll handle it."

The officers agreed to leave the situation in the sheriff's hands. It would be Sheriff Rippford's job to rebuild his town's reputation. He knew that if he didn't come up with a solution quickly, he would be under investigation himself and either lose his position or, worse yet, be put in jail. He had to come up with a plan to end it all, and fast.

The following Monday started off in the usual way. Richard went off to his job, and Pamela tended the household chores while Johnnie went to school. The kids at school were very quiet and hardly said a word all day. They didn't even talk much among themselves. At the plant, Richard tended to his duties as manager as best he could. However, he figured he was in an unsolvable situation.

That day after lunch, the sheriff asked his men to join him in the back room of his office for a secret meeting. Sheriff Rippford even locked the front door and had the jail keeper turn people away unless it was an emergency. In the back room, Rippford and his four deputies hashed out a plan to end the trouble in Creek Canyon once and for all. The plan would be carried out that very night.

When evening came, Johnnie was doing some homework, and Pamela had prepared a meal for her family. After giving thanks, the DuFours sat down to eat. Little was said at the dinner table that night. After they finished eating and clearing the table, the DuFours went into the living room to relax. As they sat near the crackling fire, they heard a sudden knock on the front door. They looked at one another.

"Now who do you suppose?" Richard said.

He rose slowly and walked into the kitchen to answer the door as a second knock came. As Richard slowly started to open the door, it burst wide open with a sudden kick. In an instant, five men pushed their way into the house with burlap bags tied over their heads with holes cut out for eyes. The five ruffians grabbed Richard around the waist, and one of them held Richard's arms behind his back. The sudden sound of a struggle caused the frightened Pamela and Johnnie to run into the kitchen to see what the matter was. When Pamela and her son saw the hooded men struggling with Richard, they started screaming, hoping to cause the men to stop the assault.

Three of the men twisted Richard every which way as they attempted to punch and kick him in the side. The struggling men crashed into the kitchen table and knocked the chairs to the floor. Richard struggled to free himself from their powerful grips while Pamela, in an attempt to help her husband, grabbed a cast iron skillet. She started swinging the skillet at the men to try to drive them away. One of the men blocked the skillet from hitting him in the head and pushed Pamela over a pail of ashes, sending her to the floor. As she fell, she hit the side of her head on the kitchen stove, rendering her unconscious.

"That'll teach ya!" he yelled at her.

Meanwhile, as Richard continued to try to escape the men's blows and kicks, little Johnnie picked up a fireplace poker and went after the men himself. One of the men grabbed the poker out of Johnnie's hands.

"Get out of the way, you little weasel!" the man yelled.

The man struck Johnnie in the head with the poker, also sending him to the floor. Richard, too, was finally knocked unconscious. During the struggle, his glasses were knocked off his face and crushed beyond repair. After the fight was over, the men were out of breath.

"What now?" one man asked.

"Don't you worry about that," the ringleader said. "We'll get rid of them somehow."

One of the younger men checked on Pamela. "I don't know about this!" he nervously said.

Then he looked at Johnnie lying on the floor with blood seeping out of his head. "We gotta get outta here!" he exclaimed.

Richard also was lying on the floor, bleeding from the struggle. The younger man started to panic. "We gotta do sumptin' fast, boys!"

Fearing that the DuFours were dead, he said to the other four men, "We didn't come here to kill them, did we?"

"It don't matter," growled one of the others. "Now we have to do something with them fast!"

"We could torch the house with them still in it," one of the men suggested.

"Nah, we can't do that," another man said. "The government would come in and swarm all over this place like bees on a honeycomb since these folks are here with that industrial program."

The five also knew that the fire marshals from Rapid City would investigate the cause of the fire, and it would be hard to make it look like an accident. The five ruffians came up with a plan. They would place the DuFour family on the two horses in the barn and lead them out into the flatlands. The plan was to make it look like the DuFours had accidentally got bucked off and were injured when they hit the ground. The five men also knew the vultures and wolves would eventually pick the lifeless family clean before anyone would find them.

And so it was that the five men draped Richard, Pamela, and little Johnnie over the horses' backs and led them out into the plains area of the Badlands of South Dakota. The men made the trip under the cover of darkness and also made sure they were miles away from the DuFours' home. Just before dawn, the five men found an area with rocks strewn on the ground and figured it would be a good place for an accident to happen.

They placed the DuFour family on the ground and then spanked the two horses, sending them running wildly into the wilderness. The sun was starting to rise above the horizon, and the party of five decided it was time to head back to town.

As the DuFours were lying on the ground, a sudden shriek could be heard up in the skies. The screech became louder and louder, bringing Richard out of unconsciousness. He slowly forced his eyes open in the morning sun and could only see blurred images. As the screeching continued, the sound seemed to pierce Richard's heart like it did before. Suddenly, his vision became sharp and clear. Even with his glasses on, Richard had never been able to see as clearly as he could at that moment. Richard thought he had died and gone to heaven because the sky was so bright. He could see the source of the screeching sounds. It was a male American bald eagle, much like the one he had seen while helping the old Indian. As he watched the graceful bird soaring above him, Richard lapsed into a trance and closed his eyes.

A little while went by as the DuFours still lay lifelessly on the ground. During the late morning, a Yankton hunting party stumbled upon the family. The hunters dismounted their horses to investigate. When they noticed that all three of the DuFour family had blood on them, the hunting party was startled, thinking it might be a setup for an ambush. A couple of the hunters scouted the area but only saw horse hoof prints that led to and from the scene in a single file. After searching the area for more evidence, the hunting party noticed the hoof prints of the horses that had run off. The group knew instantly something wasn't right and decided to see if the three were still alive.

Three of the braves drew close to Richard, Pamela, and Johnnie while the others stood watch for anyone else. One brave placed his ear on Richard's chest, listening for his heartbeat.

"This man lives!" he said in the Yankton language.

The brave who checked on Pamela slowly raised his head off of her chest and shook it back and forth. "She has no life in her," the brave said.

A third brave raised his head from Johnnie's chest and shook his head back and forth also. It was clear to the braves that Pamela and little Johnnie were dead.

CHAPTER SEVEN

Recovering with the Yankton

Despite the shocking circumstances, the Yankton hunting party decided to bring the DuFours back to their village. The Yankton braves quickly assembled a travois and suspended it from the backside of one of their horses. The tribesmen placed Richard on the travois and covered him with blankets to keep him warm. When they were done tending to Richard, the braves draped Pamela and Johnnie's bodies over a horse and covered them with a ceremonial blanket meant to ward off evil spirits.

The hunters brought the DuFours up into the mountains to their village of teepees, campfires, and makeshift racks for dressing their kill for food. While the hunting party was traveling to the village, the same bald eagle followed along with them high in the air. The bird's shrieks echoed off the mountains. The braves noticed the eagle's presence and knew it followed them to the village for a reason.

Richard started to regain consciousness, and he slowly opened his eyes once again to the bright, blue sky. When he did so, Richard saw the eagle flying high above him. To Richard, the graceful bird appeared to be projecting bright, golden rays of light. Before the others could notice that he was awake, Richard peacefully closed his eyes again and went into a deep sleep.

As the hunting party approached the village, other braves, led by Crouching Cougar, one of the tribe's best hunters, ran to find out what had happened. When the hunting party explained to Crouching Cougar how they had discovered the DuFours on the trail, he ran back to the village to summon Fighting Bear. Both Crouching Cougar and Fighting Bear ran back to the others. When Fighting Bear saw Richard, he recognized him from when Richard had tried to help their deceased comrade after the cowboys struck him down. Fighting Bear said to the others in the Yankton language, "Yes! This is the blessed one we saw!" Fighting Bear walked over to Pamela and little Johnnie and peered under the blanket. He told the others that they must have been Richard's family. Fighting Bear instructed the others to go into the village while he and Crouching Cougar ran ahead of them to summon the chief. When the hunting party arrived in the village with the DuFour family, all members of the tribe circled around them. Chief Strong Buffalo, who was named for his strength in leadership, stepped over to observe Richard.

"Will he live?" Strong Buffalo asked the tribe's newly appointed medicine man.

The medicine man examined Richard. "His wounds are many," he said. "We shall care for him, and he may live."

Strong Buffalo and the medicine man decided to place Richard in a teepee set up for the wounded, under the care of a couple of women. Then the medicine man and a spiritual leader chanted a blessing on Pamela and Johnnie's spirits for safe journey to Creator. The tribesmen placed their bodies in another teepee to be wrapped in loins soaked with ointments for preservation. The women caring for Richard cleansed his wounds with healing herbs and bandaged them to stop the bleeding. After that, the women washed the rest of Richard's body. As Richard faded in and out of consciousness, the women gave him a hot herbal drink to sip and tried to comfort him while he slowly regained his strength. Richard was still not aware what had happened to his wife and child.

A few days went by, and Richard began asking about his family. The women didn't know how to answer him, so they met with the chief and asked him what to tell Richard. The chief instructed the women to tell Richard that his wife and son were in comfort while he recovered from his wounds. The chief believed Pamela and Johnnie were indeed in comfort with Creator but didn't want Richard to know that his family was alive only in spirit.

As time went on, Richard took comfort in what the women had told him concerning his family. According to what the women had said,

Richard realized his attackers had taken he and his family out into the wilderness to die. While getting to know the women, Richard noticed that one was different from the rest. She was a short, slender woman, perhaps in her mid-thirties with long, straight, dark hair like the other women. What made her appearance unique, however, was that she had lily-white skin and greenish-hazel eyes.

One day while the other women were going about their other duties, the light-skinned woman was tending to Richard alone.

"Why aren't you a redskin like the others?" Richard asked.

"My father was an Irishman, and my mother was Yankton," the woman said.

"My father traveled to the New World from Ireland when he was young, and he traveled west for silver and gold before the Civil War broke out."

"And after the war?" Richard asked.

"After the war broke out, he decided to stay out here to work," the woman answered. "While here, Father met my mother and they were married in the Yankton tradition. From that time on, Father and Mother remained here for good."

"Wow! An Irish man mixed with a Yankton woman. Now that's a shot of whiskey!" Richard said with a laugh. It was the first time since he had been there that Richard had laughed.

"What is your name?" Richard asked.

"My name is White Deer," she told him. "I know I am getting on in years, but I choose not to marry, for times are bad now. My only hope is that someday things will be better for me to raise a family."

Richard understood that White Deer was talking about the oppression the Yankton were suffering by the miners, especially in Creek Canyon, making it hard for the tribe to live peacefully. After a couple of weeks, Richard was able to stand up and walk around, and he wanted to venture outside the teepee.

The women told the chief about Richard's good recovery. White Deer and one of the other women took Richard by the arms and led him around the village while some of the braves smiled at his progress. Richard observed how the Yankton lived. He took note of how they dressed according to their rank in life. The chief wore a long headdress filled with different types of feathers and boasted an assortment of necklaces that showed others his achievements.

The medicine man's outfit differed from the others as well, because he carried small leather pouches of herbs and other ground-up materials for healing purposes. The warriors boasted markings on their faces and bodies that revealed their position within the tribe. Richard soon realized it took hard work, time, and achievements to earn specialized articles of clothing and markings. This was a different way of life to Richard, who was used to seeing phony people playing the wealth game. Richard respected the Yankton's simple, honest ways of living.

Strong Buffalo told the women it was time for Richard to know the truth about his family. White Deer and the other women led Richard to the Yankton's lodge teepee where tribe members meditated periodically. In the middle of the teepee, a fire was lit under several large stones to keep them hot, and water was poured on top of the stones to create steam within the teepee. The two women introduced Richard to Chief Strong Buffalo and one of the tribe's spiritual leaders, who were seated around the fire.

"Please sit," the chief said.

A covering of mats made from animal skins had been placed on the ground inside the teepee to comfort them from the cold dirt floor. The natives didn't use chairs like the ones Richard was used to. Richard sat down on one of the mats opposite Chief Strong Buffalo and the spiritual leader and crossed his legs. White Deer and the other woman spoke a salutation of respect to the chief and left the lodge teepee.

The two Yankton tribe leaders were quiet for a moment as they looked upon Richard with sadness. Chief Strong Buffalo spoke first. "The Yankton people believe the spirits of nature guide us through good times and bad times as well. When one dies in the body, the spirit departs and travels to Creator to live with our ancestors," the chief said.

"Yes, I do believe as well!" Richard said. "I also believe that when a person follows God's ways, he also goes to heaven to be with the Lord for eternity."

The chief and the medicine man smiled at Richard and were pleased to hear he had a belief similar to theirs. Strong Buffalo and the medicine man fell quiet once again. Richard knew they had something to tell him about his wife and son. Richard became very sad.

"It's about my wife and son, isn't it?"

"Yes, it is," Chief Strong Buffalo said.

Richard sat for a few moments and just stared at the fire's small flames. The spiritual leader poured some water on the hot rocks to create more steam. Richard slowly lifted his head.

"Tell me, good people. Tell me what had happened."

"Your wife and son are in the comfort of Creator and are waiting to greet you when it is time for you to join them," the spiritual leader said.

"I am afraid your wife and child did not survive the attack," the chief said.

Richard, in a state of shock, took some deep breaths and closed his eyes. The two tribesmen told Richard they would leave him alone to mourn for his wife and son. And so, after the chief and the spiritual leader had left the teepee, Richard wept bitterly for Pamela and Johnnie. He was now alone in an unknown territory.

After an hour or so had passed, Richard collected himself and left the lodge teepee. He slowly walked around the tribe's village, stunned about the news of his family. Richard set off to find the chief to inquire about the bodies of Pamela and Johnnie. The chief led Richard to the medicine man, who told Richard he had wrapped the bodies in preservative loins for a proper burial.

"How do you wish your wife and son to be buried?" the medicine man asked Richard.

Richard went into deep thought for a few minutes. "Since the white man killed them, I don't want my family to be buried in the white man's ways," Richard told the medicine man. "Please bury Pamela and Johnnie in the ways of the Yankton."

The two men walked back to the chief and told him of Richard's decision so a proper burial could be arranged. Richard walked back to the teepee where he was recovering and laid down to rest from all he had learned that day. The day soon led into night, and Richard nibbled on some dried meat strips given to him by some of the tribal people and drank some water. The death of his family still weighed heavy on his heart. Richard laid back down in the darkness and drifted off to sleep in tears.

Before the late autumn sun rose the next day, the birds awoke Richard with their gentle peeps and chirps. He got out of his bed of animal skins, dressed warmly, and walked out of the teepee. Richard slowly walked down a short path to an open area overlooking the mountains to the east. There, Richard found White Deer.

"Why are you here, White Deer?" Richard asked.

"I often come here to watch the sun create a new day with new hopes to bring upon us," White Deer told Richard.

Richard didn't know what to hope for, but he respected her belief about the dawning of a new day.

"I'm having my wife and son buried in the Yankton ways," Richard told White Deer.

White Deer nodded in agreement. "That is good," she said.

As the sun rose, the chill of the late autumn air began to dissipate. Richard and White Deer walked back to the village where the others were preparing the morning meal. No blueberry flapjacks here. Instead, the meal was made from ground corn and wheat resembling grits like Pamela had made at the Creek Canyon homestead. Richard shared the meal with the rest of the villagers who had gathered to eat together. When the morning meal was done, the chief stood up and spoke to the others about the burial ceremony for Richard's family that would take place that day.

The time had come for Richard and the Yankton people to pay their respects to Pamela and Jonathan. The spiritual leaders placed Richard's wife and son's bodies on large slabs of stone and covered them with a ceremonial covering to ensure their spirits a safe journey to Creator. Chief Strong Buffalo turned to the people and spoke.

"The spirit gives the body life! Yes, the body can be destroyed by man, but the spirit lives on!" the chief said.

Strong Buffalo raised his arm and pointed to Richard. "Although this man lost his family, they will be reunited once again with Creator. It is far better to be with Creator! We should only mourn for a short time when a loved one departs." Other spiritual men lit clusters of sage grass on fire and held them in the air to ward off evil spirits. While they chanted prayers, others sounded flutes, tapped on drums, and shook rattles to say farewell to the spirits as they rose up to Creator. Richard wept and mourned for his family as he gave his wife and son one last farewell. During their burials, Richard lifted up his arms to the sky along with the others, believing his family's spirits had soared in the air like an eagle looking down from the heavens. From that time on, Richard accepted his fate in life among the Yankton people and adopted to their way of life.

Because autumn was drawing to an end, Richard had a lot to learn from his newly adopted family. Richard needed to strengthen his body to prepare for the oncoming winter. He started wearing animal skin clothing in the cold and also wearing garments woven from horsehair. He soon ventured out on hunting trips and learned the ways of hunting from Fighting Bear and Crouching Cougar.

The two hunting leaders had different styles of hunting, which made it easier for the villagers to have a good supply of food and furs. Fighting Bear was an aggressive leader who always had his group encircle buffalo or antelope herds and then close in on them by galloping their horses while yelling high-pitched shrieks. The hunting party either speared their prey or took it down by bow and arrows. Crouching Cougar, on the other hand, got his name from being like a mountain lion hiding in the grass. Crouching Cougar and his party would spot a herd of prey and dismount their horses at a distance. Slowly, the hunting party would crawl through tall grass or brush to get closer to their prey. Some of the hunters wore animal masks to camouflage themselves. Then they would jump up and take down as many animals as they could with their weapons.

Richard enjoyed the two styles of hunting, but found Crouching Cougar's method a more suitable way to hunt. As he became more successful at hunting, he accumulated the tribal markings that boasted of his achievements. As time passed, he was soon able to train as a warrior.

As the South Dakotan winter arrived with its bitter chill, the villagers had enough dried food to sustain them and only had to hunt occasionally to maintain the supply of fresh meat. They also fished in the unfrozen portions of nearby streams for a treat of stream trout. The Yankton people lodged together quite often to refresh their spirituality and lit a large outdoor fire to huddle around on days it didn't snow. During the winter, Richard would demonstrate to the other warriors how to strengthen themselves by repeatedly running through deep snow. Richard also trained some warriors by having them climb a thirty-foot-high cliff with ropes.

Richard also taught the tribe various upper-body strengthening exercises by lifting stones and logs. The former chemical engineer even devised a way to do push-ups with one end of a long log resting on the ground and the other end resting on his back. As he gained strength, Richard increased the size of the log. He also taught some of the braves how to swing side to side from the cliff suspended by ropes while working their way down from the top. Richard learned how to throw spears and hit small targets, as well as the Yankton's way of archery. With all the short hunting and fishing trips, and all the new outdoor sports Richard taught them, the Yankton people were surprised at how fast winter seemed to be passing.

By winter's end, Richard had strengthened his body much more than what it ever was before. One day after Richard was done with his push-ups, he rose slowly, flexing his strong muscles, and said to those around him, "The time is drawing near for me to go and fight!"

The warriors knew Richard had unfinished business back in town. The days grew warmer and the snow melted away. Richard had let his hair and beard grow throughout the winter for warmth. But now with spring approaching, he wanted the beard trimmed, so he asked some of the braves to trim his beard with sharp knives.

On one warm day, Richard heard the familiar sound of pots and pans clanging together and the gleeful singing of a joyous man coming up the pathway to the village. It was Richard's friend Daniel. Some of the braves went down to greet Daniel as the mountain man approached. Richard slipped into a teepee nearby to watch his friend and his donkey be greeted by the others. Daniel often ventured up to the village when the weather cooperated and when he had food or other items to trade for articles of clothing.

Richard hadn't seen Daniel since before the struggle with the five men, and his heart beat vigorously as he watched the man. While Daniel was standing by his donkey waiting to see what he could trade, Richard went out to greet him. He stepped out of the teepee and walked toward Daniel. Daniel didn't recognize Richard with his long hair and beard. He thought Richard was someone new to trade with. Richard paused and yelled out, "Dan, the nature man!"

Daniel was stunned to hear a stranger call him by his nickname, and as Richard drew closer, Daniel's eyes grew wide in disbelief. "Is that who I think it is?"

"Sure is, ole fella!" Richard shouted.

He and Daniel laughed as they embraced. After a few minutes, Daniel suddenly grew quiet, and Richard asked, "It's the townspeople, right?"

Daniel nodded his head. "Rumor has it that you and your family went out on a horseback ride and never returned."

Daniel had a very sad expression on his face as he continued. "A few days later, your two horses were found roaming around the town. The sheriff had told the townspeople that a search party was sent out to look for you all, and a report came back saying that all three of ya's had been found dead from a horse-riding accident."

Richard shook his head in disbelief.

"My friend, the sheriff even claimed that your bodies had been picked apart by animals and were too decomposed to bring them back to town!" Daniel said.

Daniel took a deep breath and sighed. "Then that blasted sheriff had the nerve to say he had the remains sent back East to your own families!"

"I had found out earlier the sheriff was behind all of this all along, my friend," Richard said.

"I was very sad to hear the news about you all being dead, but I had no way to see for myself without being gunned down," Daniel told Richard.

"I understand your position, ole fellow," Richard said. "What really happened was that some men knocked on my front door one evening, and when I went to open it, they pushed their way in!"

Richard looked Daniel in the eye. "They all grabbed a hold of me and knocked me to the floor! I do remember hearing Pamela and Johnnie screaming and yelling, but that's all I can remember until I woke up here."

For some time, Richard had been trying to think of a way to go back to Creek Canyon and face the sheriff. Now that he had the testimony of his trusted friend, Richard knew he had to square things away with the sheriff and the four deputies.

"How do the townspeople treat you, my friend?" Richard asked Daniel.

"Oh, they usually just laugh at me and sometimes poke fun at the animal skins I wear or how I travel with my old donkey here," Daniel said.

"Would you feel safe enough to buy some clothes for me in town?" Richard asked.

"Sure, my friend," Daniel said. "Why, I could even do it without any questions from anybody."

Then Richard asked Daniel to do one other favor.

"Yes, anything," Daniel said.

Richard told Daniel where he and his family had hidden some money in some canning jars under a stone behind the house. Richard told him which stone to look for and to use the money to buy western-style boots, pants, leather chaps, and a leather vest. Richard also asked his trusted friend to purchase a cowboy hat and a lever-action rifle with plenty of ammunition. Daniel said he would do the best he could, and Richard told him to keep the rest of the money for himself.

And with that, Daniel completed his dealings with the Yankton people and left with his supplies and Richard's request.

*   *   *   *

Back in Creek Canyon, it was business as usual. The nitroglycerine plant was in full operation, and the saloons were booming with activity. Daniel arrived in town as he always had with his pots and pans clanging. As usual, some of the men and even a few women and children laughed at him when he strolled into town with his donkey and tinny symphony. Daniel, ignoring them, just whistled a tune and went into the shops to buy the items Richard had requested. Some of the store clerks were a bit surprised to see Daniel buying clothes and boots for the first time in a long time. One of them even laughed and asked the mountain man if he had struck it rich somewhere. Daniel just told them he had sold some furs he had trapped and saved up his money.

Daniel went into the gun shop, which had an assortment of pistols and rifles and a good supply of ammunition.

"Hey, you. Aren't you the one who lives by nature up in the mountains?" the shop owner asked as Daniel looked around.

"Yep, that's me alright," Daniel said. "I had lots of trouble finding food this year, and I need a gun to hunt with during the cold winter months come next year. Now, if you would be ever so kind to tells me which one of these here rifles is the best one around, I would be much obliged."

The gun shop owner showed Daniel an assortment of the newest rifles. After asking some more questions about the rifles, Daniel chose the finest lever-action rifle that money could buy. It was a Winchester repeater lever-action rifle put out in 1866. He also purchased what seemed to be a season's worth of ammunition. After Daniel had completed his shopping, he left Creek Canyon.

CHAPTER EIGHT

Richard's Plan of Action

While Daniel was in town, Richard explained his plan to the chief about going up against the sheriff and the four deputies who had taken part in the killings of his wife and son. The chief took council with Fighting Bear and Crouching Cougar about Richard's plan. The three Yankton tribesmen told Richard he was going to be a brave warrior by facing the cold-hearted killers. The spiritual leader blessed Richard, asking the spirits to watch over him while he ventured back down to Creek Canyon. A day later, Daniel returned to the village with Richard's supplies.

"Thank you my friend," Richard said. "Can you do me just one more favor?" "Sure can!" Daniel said.

"Can you ask someone in town to see if the sheriff still has any more of his evil plans?" Richard asked.

"Sure will!" Daniel said. "Who?"

"Okay," Richard said. "Go to the telegram operator and tell him I sent you there."

"What dealings do you have with that ole boy?" Daniel asked.

"He's got information on the sheriff and his men that you should know about," Richard said.

"You got it my friend!" Daniel said.

Daniel went on his way toward town. After he had arrived in Creek Canyon, he went into the telegram office and told the operator how he had found Richard.

The operator was surprised to hear that Richard was still alive and told Daniel the same information he had told Richard months ago. After his visit at the telegram office, Daniel discreetly made his way around town to see if he could find out anything new.

Richard decided to wait until the next day to approach the sheriff and his men. He spent the rest of the night sitting around a fire listening to the elders tell stories of their ancestors. As the old men told their tales of dreams and visions, Richard remembered the visions he had concerning the hydro dam and knew it was time to find out the truth about the matter.

Richard raised his hand. "Strong Buffalo? Would you and the other leaders tell me what my visions mean?"

"Speak and we shall hear what it is," the spiritual leader said. The whole group grew quiet.

"All of my visions started back East when I first saw the diagram of the dam," Richard said.

When Richard mentioned the dam, the older men grew more attentive. They realized that Richard was speaking about the hydro dam that the Yankton people referred to as "The Wall of Death."

"I heard faint cries and yelling as I looked at the diagram while at my brother-in-law's place in New York City," he said.

The older men nodded their heads in acknowledgement.

"When I visited the dam, I fell to the ground in a trance," Richard said.

"I had visions of people crying and screaming as they floated in floodwaters!

Why, my people, did I have such visions?"

"You are a chosen one," one older man said.

"It was not too many moons ago that the Wall of Death was constructed."

He looked intently at Richard. "The white man wanted to build a dam to power their operations. But, by building it, the water would flood the plains and our village behind the dam as it filled up. The small river that once ran through the narrow canyon was to be made into a reservoir," the aged man said.

After the aged man stopped speaking, Chief Strong Buffalo drew closer to Richard's face. "The chiefs had made a treaty with the miners so they would not build a dam as large as they had wanted to. We agreed to move our village farther away from the shore, but while the dam was being built, we saw it was much larger than agreed to in the treaty."

Everyone around the campfire remained quiet as the chief spoke. Only the crickets, katydids, and the crackling fire were the sounds to be heard.

"The builders of the dam told us they were going to keep the iron floodgates open to keep the water level low. That way there, we didn't need to move our village too far inland. The builders also told us that the dam had to be large and strong in case of a flash flood."

Richard stared at the tribesmen while he listened to their story, but the old wise men had more to tell. The medicine man went on to tell Richard about the most heartbreaking event he had ever heard.

"One night after the dam was built and when the moon was full, the miners snuck up to it and lowered the large iron floodgates to close off the river. The water rose silently to the tops of the riverbanks that night and overflowed into our village," the medicine man said.

"As the waters rushed into the village, it was too late to escape the gripping currents of the flood. The water swept away the teepees, taking the lives of many men, women, and children."

The women, including White Deer, had tears streaming down their faces. "People cried and screamed as they frantically tried to save themselves and those around them. Some of the villagers survived by clinging to large branches and floating to dry land. Some of the survivors were children who lost their parents; other survivors were parents who lost their children," the medicine man said.

The aged men also told Richard that they believed the spirits of the people who drowned in the flooded reservoir were still trapped beneath the waters. "That was how the dam became known to the Yankton people as the Wall of Death," he said.

Richard's heart sank as he heard the story.

"I have heard of such killings from the mouths of the miners themselves!" Richard told the tribesmen.

"The miners boasted of killings, hangings, and even torture to the natives when they opposed anything they did. I heard something about a massive drowning too. I hadn't realized how the miners intentionally flooded a village to wipe the people out by drowning them though!" Richard said.

The Yankton people told Richard that Creek Canyon had the worst reputation for murdering natives in all the land. Richard asked his fellow tribesmen if any of them had survived that night.

The old men all raised their hands. "We lost wives and children along with brothers and sisters that horrible night," one old man said.

Then some of the younger members raised their hands. "We lost mothers and fathers that night as well."

Crouching Cougar told how he lost his parents in the flood and went on to learn how to survive on his own by hunting and fishing. "I became a fierce but silent warrior because of what happened to me!" Crouching Cougar said.

After Crouching Cougar told his tale, White Deer asked to speak. The men gave her permission. "I, too, had lost my mother and father, whom I told you about earlier, Richard," White Deer said.

Richard realized something serious had to be done very soon. After the stories were over, the villagers got up and returned to their teepees for the night. Only White Deer and Richard remained by the fire. They both sat back down again and that's when Richard told her of his plan of action. White Deer became worried for Richard, but she knew he had to do what he needed to do. White Deer returned to her teepee, and Richard went to his teepee but he had a hard time getting to sleep. Richard kept going over the stories in his mind until he finally drifted off to sleep.

The next morning, Richard got up while it was still dark and walked down to the overlook to watch the sun rise. Richard was alone and had time to meditate and chant some of the spiritual chants he had learned while living with the Yankton. After Richard ate the morning meal with the rest of the tribe, he started to prepare for his first trip into town since the meeting in the town hall. Richard took off his Yankton outfit and put on the western clothing Daniel had bought for him. Richard climbed on his horse and set off to town dressed as a cowboy. The only unusual features were the tribal achievement markings he'd left on his face and arms. White Deer wiped some tears away from her face as she watched him leave.

The day was hot and dry, and the townspeople were going about their daily business. One man saw Richard's shimmering figure among the heat waves as he approached on horseback. As Richard drew closer to the town, more and more people noticed him. When he entered the town, the townspeople were perplexed at the stranger dressed as a cowboy, yet having long hair and Indian markings on his face. People stared as they tried to figure out who he was or, better yet, *what* he was.

Richard stopped at the jailhouse where the sheriff's office was. He dismounted his horse and went inside to confront the sheriff, but neither the sheriff nor his men were there. When Richard inquired about the sheriff, the jail keeper told him the men were at the saloon across the street. Richard left the jailhouse, unhitched his horse, and crossed the dusty street to the saloon.

Richard could hear a piano playing as he approached. When he walked through the swinging doors, the patrons noticed the stranger right away. The whiskey drinkers also took notice of the markings on Richard's face and arms when he walked by them. As the men grew silent, someone stopped the player piano's drum from playing. By now, everyone was staring at the man, wondering if he was a cowboy or an Indian.

"So, who might you be? A cowboy or an Injun?" one of the patrons finally asked Richard.

"Maybe he's got both blood in him!" another older man said.

"If he's got but one drop of Injun blood in him, he ain't no cowboy!" a third man shouted.

Suddenly, an uproar broke out in the saloon, much like it had in the town hall.

Another man stood up. "What business do you got around here, mister?" he yelled.

"I got business with the sheriff!" Richard snapped back.

The sheriff was sitting at the bar watching what was going on. When Richard spoke, the sheriff recognized his voice, and Rippford's eyes grew wide. The deputies also recognized Richard's voice.

Richard stared at the sheriff and his men. "Sheriff! You and your men are going to pay for the crimes committed against the Yankton tribe and my family!"

Rippford and his deputies wanted to shoot Richard right then and there but feared there were too many witnesses around and rumors might get back to Rapid City. The sheriff gritted his teeth.

"I will do all I can to help you, Mr. DuFour," he said.

When the other patrons heard that, they gasped and exchanged shocked looks with one another.

"Well, if that's so, Rippford, then you and your men can start helping me by locking yourselves up in the jail right now!" Richard hollered.

"Very well then!" Rippford grumbled. "We'll see about all this!"

The sheriff and his men got up, walked out of the saloon, and went across the street to the jailhouse. Richard, feeling defenseless, mounted his horse with the intention of riding to Rapid City the following day. While the others looked on, Richard rode out of town.

CHAPTER NINE

Eagle Eye

Sheriff Rippford realized his plan had backfired on him. He now had to come up with yet another plan to rid his town of the ever-persistent Richard DuFour. Part of the sheriff's plan had worked because Pamela and Jonathan had died, but Richard, who was the main problem in the sheriff's eyes, still remained. The sheriff decided to get the whole town involved in getting rid of Richard this time around. The next day, Rippford had "Wanted" posters printed with a five hundred dollar reward placed on Richard's head. He and the deputies tacked up the posters up all over town.

The posters stated Richard had turned into a madman and had slain his family in the wilderness. Other falsified reports stated that Richard had hidden in the mountains for the winter and decided to come back to Creek Canyon to blame his crimes on the sheriff and the deputies.

Soon, the posters with a drawing of Richard's face were the talk of the town. A five hundred dollar reward was no small change, and each person wanted to be the victorious hero to bring in the sheriff's prize.

One day as Daniel was in town buying supplies, he spotted one of the posters. After talking with some of the townspeople and the telegram operator, Daniel learned there was going to be a massive manhunt for Richard. Daniel ripped down one of the posters and left town without saying anything else to anyone. When Daniel was out of sight, he raced to the Yankton village to warn Richard.

*　　*　　*　　*

At the village, Richard was preparing to set off to Rapid City as planned. The former engineer was just about to mount his horse when he heard his name being called out over and over again. It was Daniel! This time, the mountain man hadn't arrived in his usual manner of singing with his pots and pans clanging like a bunch of cowbells. Richard knew something was wrong when he saw his old friend running toward him out of breath. Daniel could hardly speak when he got to Richard, and he fell on his knees trying to catch his breath.

Richard and a couple of braves helped Daniel up to see what the matter was. After Daniel caught his breath, he showed Richard one of the "Wanted" posters. "These "Wanted" posters are all over town for your capture!" Daniel said gasping for air.

"Look, there's even a five hundred dollar reward on your head!"

"The sheriff is now blaming *you* for killing your own family!" he told Richard.

"I also heard that there's going to be a massive manhunt to flush you out of the mountains to capture you dead or alive!"

The news concerned Richard greatly and infuriated him at the same time.

Richard slowly crumpled up the poster and remained silent.

"And, to top it all off, everything I heard was true according to that old telegram operator," Daniel added.

Richard realized once again he was a target of the townspeople. He also knew that eventually, the Yankton village would be invaded and attacked, if necessary, for his capture. Richard decided not to go to Rapid City, but instead, to try to avoid the massive manhunt for him.

"I have no choice but to face the sheriff and the deputies once again myself to protect the Yankton tribe from invasion," Richard told the chief.

Chief Strong Buffalo, the spiritual leaders, and the two head warriors got together. The group of tribal leaders wanted to hold a powwow with the other braves concerning Richard's act of bravery. The chief asked Richard to let them conduct the powwow without his presence. Richard agreed to go somewhere quiet to focus on finding peace with himself.

Richard told Daniel to keep a low profile because he had no idea what would happen in town. The two friends parted ways. Richard rode up to a cliff facing west this time, to a spot that was peaceful and quiet. While there, Richard meditated and chanted prayers to Creator in the Yankton language and his own language as well.

As Richard prayed, he felt a blanket of security drape over him, and a very peaceful, warm feeling flowed right through him. Suddenly, Richard was startled by the shrill of an eagle's cry! To Richard, it seemed to be the very same eagle he'd been seeing since the day he had helped the fallen Yankton man on the road. Richard looked up at the graceful bald eagle and saw its celestial body with golden rays projecting from it as before. The eagle seemed to be giving him power of some kind as Richard sat and stared at the bird gliding through the air.

When his experience had passed, Richard realized that not only could he still see clearly with no glasses, a strange sense of sight had come into his right eye. With his right eye, Richard could focus on objects as easily as an eagle can spot a mouse from hundreds of feet in the air. Richard knew he had been given some kind of mystical power for a specific reason.

*   *   *   *

Back at the village, the chief, the spiritual leader and the medicine man waited for Richard's return.

"The warriors want to help you solve the matter with the sheriff by going into Creek Canyon with you," the chief informed Richard. "They want to try to talk to the sheriff about what could be done to avoid more bloodshed."

Richard thought about what the chief had said, but for the first time since living with the Yankton, Richard disagreed with the tribesmen's decision.

"I must face the sheriff and his men alone," Richard told them. "Rippford and his men ganged up on me and my family, and now, my wife and son are dead!"

Strong Buffalo, the spiritual leader, and the medicine man honored Richard's wishes but were very concerned for him. This time, Richard was preparing to go to war instead of going to the sheriff in peace. As the chief looked at Richard gravely, Richard told him of his gift of vision from the eagle and decided to demonstrate to the others that he was not imagining things.

"Have some of your braves hide in the surrounding area, out of view, to see if I can find them," Richard suggested to the chief.

It seemed to be like a hide-and-seek game from Richard's youth, but this time, it was for battle reasons.

"Go into your teepee while I have some of the braves find hiding places," the chief instructed Richard.

After about fifteen minutes or so, the chief called out for Richard to seek and find the braves. As Richard walked down into a small gorge in the mountains, his right eye was zooming in and out of areas where a man could possibly hide.

He soon spotted one brave high on a cliff in a crevice obscured behind a tree. Richard called out to the brave by name and had him return to the village. Richard went on a little farther and spotted another brave hiding in a small den in the rocks and called out to the brave by his name. Like the first brave, Richard instructed him to go back to the village as well.

After a while, Richard walked through a thick, wooded area and spotted a deer, owls, raccoons, and other wildlife. Richard approached a thicket of pines where he spotted Fighting Bear.

"Come down and walk with me, Fighting Bear!" Richard yelled.

Fighting Bear was astonished at Richard's eyesight and walked with him as Richard had asked. The two of them entered a clearing of tall grass and some thick scrub brush. Richard pointed to a cluster of bushes and said to Fighting Bear, "Look over there! It's Crouching Cougar!"

Fighting Bear tried to see what Richard was pointing to but saw nothing.

Richard called out to Crouching Cougar, "Emerge from your hiding place, Crouching Cougar!"

Sure enough, Crouching Cougar slowly stood up and revealed himself; he was just as astonished at Richard's eyesight as Fighting Bear was. The three warriors walked back to the village. Along the way, Richard kept pointing out small birds to the other two braves to demonstrate his keen eyesight.

*   *   *   *

Back at the village, the chief met up with Richard, Fighting Bear, and Crouching Cougar.

"Richard spotted the other two braves very easily," Chief Strong Buffalo said. "This man has special eyesight sight and found us as well!" Crouching Cougar said.

Fighting Bear added, "He not only found us, but he spotted other wildlife."

Chief Strong Buffalo realized Richard had indeed been blessed with the eye of an eagle. Richard called for a meeting of the minds with Chief Strong Buffalo, Fighting Bear, Crouching Cougar, and the village's spiritual leaders. The six of them listened to Richard's plan for going back down to Creek Canyon. Richard would be dressing as a cowboy once again. This time, however, he planned to wear a quiver across his back. The quiver was not going to be used for holding arrows but for the rifle Daniel had bought for him. The Yankton tribesmen honored Richard's bravery and chanted a blessing for the spirits to oversee his conquest.

That night at the evening meal, the air was still, and little was said about the next day's events. After everyone had eaten a meal of roasted antelope, the villagers said goodnight, and Richard went alone to his teepee for a good night's rest.

The next morning, Richard rose with the birds to observe the dawning of a new day. When he walked down to the east cliff to watch the sun rise, Richard met up with White Deer who was also viewing the rising sun. Richard sat down next to her.

"Today is the day I must fight my enemy," Richard said to her. White Deer didn't answer.

"This enemy is the one who destroyed my family and your ancestors and is now planning to destroy us all once again," he told her.

White Deer slowly turned and looked at him. "The eagle followed *you* here to give you power. Now, you must follow the *eagle* back to use it."

Richard knew that White Deer's simple words were true. "May this day bring you wellness," Richard said.

He got up and walked back to the village for the morning meal. After the meal, Richard was ready to face his foe. Before Richard mounted his horse, Chief Strong Buffalo, Fighting Bear, and Crouching Cougar placed their hands upon Richard's head and said to him, "May the great and mighty spirits be with you in battle."

Richard, honored by the three brave leaders, mounted his horse and slowly rode out of the village as the villagers looked on. White Deer hid among the trees once again and watched Richard leave on his brave journey to battle the enemy who had nearly killed him just nine months ago.

As the day wore on, the sun grew hotter, but Richard pressed onward toward Creek Canyon. Like before, as he drew near the town, some of the people noticed Richard as a blurred figure in the shimmering heat waves flowing along the ground. They waited to see who this shimmering figure was.

Before he reached the mining town, Richard dismounted his horse and tied it to a bush. Those who spotted Richard far off scurried away to hide. Then Richard walked right down the middle of Main Street. Despite the reward money offered by the sheriff, a couple more men were frightened by Richard's appearance. The men ran to warn the sheriff that Richard DuFour was back in town. Sensing this, Richard crossed to the side of the street opposite of the jailhouse and stood on the porch of a saloon.

The sheriff walked out to face Richard while his deputies went to take cover. Some of the deputies hid behind barrels and watering troughs; others hid on rooftops to cover the sheriff from above. All the deputies were in their places with their guns aimed at Richard. Richard and the sheriff stood across from each other, glaring. Richard spoke first.

"I'm going to give you and your men one last chance to turn yourselves in to the law in Rapid City for the crimes you've committed!"

"The crimes *we* committed? You got it all wrong there, boy!" the sheriff growled back. "*You* are the one who killed your own family, remember?"

Sheriff Rippford drew his gun from its holster. As he did, Richard drew his Winchester rifle up and out of the arrow quiver with one hand. The marksman DuFour whipped the rifle around to the front of him while cocking and loading it at the same time. Rippford was surprised at what he saw.

"End this whole ordeal at once and give yourself over to the law before somebody gets shot," the sheriff told Richard.

"The only way to end the bloodshed is for you and all the others guilty of murdering the Indians to be jailed or hung!" Richard yelled.

The sheriff stood motionless with his pistol pointing at Richard. Richard stood pointing his rifle at the sheriff. Neither one said a word. Then, suddenly, the sheriff fired his pistol, barely missing Richard's head. Rippford quickly turned his back to Richard and ran away from him. The yellow-bellied sheriff shouted a command to his men: "Take him down boys!" The cowardly sheriff ran straight back into the jailhouse to take cover.

The gun battle was on! The deputies fired shots from their hiding places on the rooftops, from behind barrels and from behind the watering troughs. Bullets were flying everywhere! Bullets were hitting the porch post Richard was standing behind, sending splinters of wood down onto him! Some of the bullets hit the saloon's windows behind Richard, sending shards of glass back at him! The smell of gun smoke drifted out into the streets and filled the air.

Richard was rapidly cocking and firing his lever-action rifle in an impressive end-over-end fashion as he returned shots to the deputies. As the gunfire grew more dangerous, Richard dove behind a water trough while dodging ricocheting bullets. The men in the saloon bailed out the back door, leaving the saloon empty.

As the shots were being fired, Richard used his right eye to focus on where the men were hiding. Richard spotted one man across the way behind a wagon and quickly took aim and shot him. Richard cocked his gun with a very quick circular motion and reloaded it while zooming in on another man and shot him also. Meanwhile, as shots were being fired from all directions, Richard jumped up and dove behind a wooden rain barrel. The gunfighter DuFour spotted another man behind a trough across the street. Richard's eye zoomed in on him, and he took the man out with one quick shot. The other deputies were up on rooftops shooting down at Richard, and he sprang up from behind the barrel, which was spewing water through the bullet holes. Richard dove through the front window of the saloon to take cover below its windowsill.

Meanwhile, the sheriff ran for the telegram office and burst through the door. "Operator! Wire a message to Robert Slinger of the Union Army stationed in Silver City right now!"

The general of the Union Army, Robert Slinger, was a personal friend of the former General George A. Custer. General Slinger's lifelong mission was to rid the newly expanding nation of Indians and make way for settlers and their opportunities. The sheriff wanted General Slinger to bring a company of soldiers to Creek Canyon to get rid of the Yankton people once and for all. The sheriff told the telegram operator the town was under attack by the Yankton tribesmen. He demanded that a wire be sent to Silver City requesting the presence of General Slinger and his men as soon as possible.

"But ain't you fellas just fighting that Richard DuFour guy?" the operator asked.

The sheriff drew his pistol out and pressed it against the back of the operator's skull.

"Listen here, old boy! You send what I tells you to send, ya hear?" he said.

"Now, I want you to send a wire to Silver City saying we are under attack by a hundred Indians, and we need General Slinger and his men here as soon as possible!" Rippford ordered. "You got that, ole boy?"

"Y-y-yes, sir," the operator said.

"Good!" the sheriff growled. He walked out of the office, disappearing out of sight and leaving his men to fend for themselves.

*   *   *   *

Back on Main Street, while three deputies continued to riddle the saloon with bullets, Richard took aim at one of them on the jailhouse roof. Richard fired a fatal shot, and the man's body toppled from the rooftop onto the ground. Richard once again zoomed in on another deputy on top of the general store, waiting patiently for the man to rise slightly to try to shoot him. The man rose. Richard shot first. The deputy's lifeless body fell onto the top of the porch below and bounced to the ground. Now the battle was down to just Richard and one last deputy.

The last deputy jumped from one rooftop to another, making it difficult for Richard to focus on him. The gunshots ceased from both as the last deputy scurried to the back of a building and slid down an outside stovepipe. Richard dashed across the street to intercept the man and end this fierce fight once and for all. As Richard crept through an alleyway behind the buildings, the deputy snuck through another alleyway.

"Come on out and let's see what you're really made of!" the deputy yelled. Richard heard the deputy's taunting call once more before he emerged from the alley. When Richard slowly went out to meet him, the deputy had his pistol in his hand pointing at the ground. Richard followed suit with his rifle. The two men walked slowly toward one another.

"If you put your gun down, so will I," the deputy said.

Richard slowly set his rifle down on the ground, not taking his eyes off the man and slowly rose up empty-handed. Surprisingly, the deputy did the same.

They both slowly stepped away from the guns.

"The sheriff will get you, sooner or later! So give yourself up!" the deputy told Richard.

"Oh yeah? Is that why he abandoned all you men?" Richard asked.

The deputy didn't say anything; he knew Richard had a point. The deputy drew his fists and approached Richard; he threw a punch. Richard quickly blocked the man's fist and threw a punch back, striking the deputy under the eye.

The lawman lunged at Richard and punched him in the ribs. He managed to knock Richard to the ground by tripping him. The deputy continued to kick Richard while he was defenseless.

Richard rolled to one side and drove a foot between the deputy's ankles, sending him to the ground. The two men wrestled and rolled around in the middle of the street while curious onlookers peeked from doorways and windows. The two men punched each other back down as they tried to stand up.

Richard was getting the best of the deputy so, in an instant, the deputy made a run for his gun. Just as the deputy picked up his pistol to shoot Richard, Richard did a swan dive onto his rifle and flipped over onto his back. Richard went into a barrel roll to escape the deputy's deadly bullets. The deputy fired a shot and grazed Richard's left shoulder. Before the deputy could shoot again, Richard finished the battle with a shot through the evil lawman's heart. The deputy's lifeless body fell to the ground with a hollow thud.

The townspeople were in shock at what they had just witnessed. At first, they remembered Richard as a mild-mannered, well-educated man—a peacekeeper.

Now, they viewed him as a revengeful, rifle-wielding vigilante, killing those who did him wrong.

The four men with the bullet holes in their hats were among the onlookers. They seemed to show up everywhere Richard went! The battle between Richard and the deputies was no exception. Richard turned to the four men and said, "Now, I don't know where your cowardly sheriff, is but you boys had better tell him I'm not finished with him yet!"

The four men nodded their heads, spat out some chewing tobacco, and walked away. The people of Creek Canyon realized they all had played a part in what had happened that day, in one way or another.

Richard went to the telegram office to wire Rapid City about the gunfight. At first, the operator didn't recognize Richard with his long hair and cowboy appearance. Only when Richard said he wanted to wire a message did the man recognize the sound of Richard's voice. He then told Richard that he had already received a message from Silver City.

"General Robert Slinger and his men are catching the next military train to Creek Canyon," the telegram operator told Richard. "The Union Army plans to declare war against the Yankton who had no part in all of this here in Creek Canyon."

Richard gave the telegram operator a very stern look. "My old friend," he said. "I don't know what's going to go down here in Hell Town, but if I were you, I'd get out of here as soon as possible and never look back!"

"Yes sir!" the operator said.

The sheriff's iron grip of unruliness in his own town had ended. Word quickly got around town about the upcoming arrival of the general's men and of the battle that was about to take place against the Yankton tribe of the Badlands. Richard knew he stood no chance against the Army and left town immediately to warn his newly adopted people.

That night, the Yankton tribe held a special ceremony for Richard. The villagers gathered around to participate in dances of blessing and to witness the welcoming of a new name for Richard. One of the Yankton artisans inked a special mark around Richard's right eye. The mark was an image of feathers, mimicking the feathers around an eagle's eye. Another mark was inked on Richard's forehead. It was shaped like an eye with a squiggly line through it—like the one drawn by the old medicine man who had died. While drums beat in the background and the spiritual men sang, the chief raised his hands and made a declaration to all the villagers present that night.

"This is Eagle Eye, for he has been blessed to see things we cannot see and to help protect us from harm!" Strong Buffalo yelled.

Then Chief Strong Buffalo blessed Richard with new warrior's markings on his arms and feathers in a headband. Everyone cheered for Richard who was now to be called Eagle Eye. The next day, Eagle Eye, Fighting Bear, Crouching Cougar, and some of the other brave warriors would face their fiercest enemy, Creek Canyon.

CHAPTER TEN

Jericho!

Chief Strong Buffalo knew that the Yankton tribes in the surrounding area had very little time to group together to fight against the powerful weapons of the Union Army. Eagle Eye, Fighting Bear, and Crouching Cougar came up with a plan to hopefully end all the strife once and for all. Eagle Eye still remembered the whole layout of the nitroglycerine plant and the hydro dam situated well above the town. The three warriors had no time to spare. They gathered all the other warriors and went over their plans.

Before the warriors left the village, Eagle Eye noticed the traditional affectionate way the warriors would depart from their loved ones to go into battle. The man would touch the woman's face on each side and rub his nose upon the woman's forehead as a farewell. As Eagle Eye mounted his horse, he sensed that someone wanted to see him off as well. Eagle Eye slowly turned around to look behind him and saw White Deer looking intently at him. Eagle Eye paused for a moment, dismounted his horse, and walked over to her. As they gazed into each other's eyes, he touched White Deer's face in the same affectionate manner. Eagle Eye tenderly kissed her on the forehead instead of rubbing his nose as his own way of saying farewell. Eagle Eye walked back to his horse and mounted it to ride off with the others to carry out their duties.

The first target in the plan was the nitroglycerin plant. Eagle Eye and his group of warriors snuck down to the plant and surrounded it. The warriors shouted battle cries, causing the workers inside the office to think they were under attack. The men in the office raced through the plant yelling to the others they were under attack. While the workers in the plant were scrambling for cover, Eagle Eye slipped into the rear entrance and made his way to the main boiler room.

Without anyone seeing him, Eagle Eye stoked up the burner box with coal and opened the air dampers to get the coals to burn red-hot. After the coals heated up, the large burner box started to boil the water in the water chamber. When the water produced more and more steam, the pressure in the accumulator tank built up rapidly. Before the pressure-relief valve had a chance to blow off steam and sound its loud whistle, Eagle Eye grabbed a ladder and a mallet along with a wooden peg used to join beams together. He set the ladder up against the accumulator and climbed up to the pressure-relief valve located near the top.

When he was near the valve, Eagle Eye took the peg and hammered it into the valve and plugged it off. After climbing back down, Eagle Eye found a wrench and twisted off the large square nut that held the hand-cranked steel wheel in place. Eagle Eye removed the wheel so no one could open the emergency valve to release the steam pressure.

*   *   *   *

In town, the sheriff had recruited the four men with the holes in their hats after hearing Richard's message. When the group of men reached the plant, another battle began. The warriors shot arrows at the cowboys to keep them at bay, and the sheriff commanded his four men to fight back. Soon, the warriors killed all four of the men in defense and the cowardly sheriff fled back into town, leaving the plant workers behind to fend for themselves.

After the Yanktons' victory, the stage was set, and Eagle Eye had one last dangerous task: to get the warriors out of the area before anyone else was killed. On his way out of the plant, Eagle Eye threw the steel wheel down a well shaft so no one could find it. Because Eagle Eye knew the plant's floor plan, he grabbed some sticks of dynamite, a hand-operated detonator, and a roll of ignition wire. Eagle Eye darted out of the plant and placed the supplies on his horse. He summoned his warriors with an eagle-sounding screech, the signal to retreat to the hills. The warriors gathered together in safety, waiting for what would happen next.

*   *   *   *

Back at the nitro plant, after the workers thought it was safe, they went inside to see if there were any more Indians inside and to inspect for any damage. The men found no signs of forced entry, no damage to the plant, and no intruders. When a boiler operator walked into the boiler room, however, he saw the twenty-foot-tall accumulator tank overloading with steam. The large accumulator was making a loud rumbling sound as it rocked back and forth under the tremendous amount of pressure.

"Oh, my God!" he yelled.

He looked up at the pressure-relief valve and noticed it was plugged off with the wooden peg. Steam was rapidly building up more and more pressure! While the accumulator continued to rock back and forth, the rumbling sound grew even louder as the steam started pushing through the accumulator's riveted plates. The rocking motion also shook the large, iron-riveted pipes leading in and out of the tank. The frightened boiler man went to manually release the steam and saw that the valve's wheel was missing! The operator knew the plant had been sabotaged. The man ran out of the room as fast as he could.

"She's gonna blow! She's gonna blow!" he yelled to his coworkers.

As the boiler man ran down the center of the plant yelling, some of the workers heard him and ran out also. Others, however, were totally unaware of the potentially dangerous situation. Then the accumulator tank exploded! With one huge burst of steam, the explosion ripped through the walls of the room. As the feed pipes burst on impact, the pipes transporting the liquid nitroglycerine also ruptured under the explosion's intense power. The highly flammable and unstable nitroglycerine ignited from the bursting pipes and started a chain reaction that was to be the largest manufacturing disaster on the western frontier.

The nitro plant continued to explode in all directions as the powerful flames ripped through the nitroglycerine pipes, shredding them to pieces and destroying the wooden ductwork. The large fire plume quickly reached the stockroom where gunpowder and a large stock of dynamite were being stored. Suddenly, the rest of the plant was blown to smithereens as it all went up in a huge ball of fire. The outer walls of the plant exploded out in all directions as the roof exploded upward. The bricked smokestacks' foundations were rocked by the blast, and the tall stacks crashed to the ground with a thunderous thud.

The townspeople were shocked by the impact of the explosion that shook the ground like a powerful earthquake. Some of the men shook their heads and said, "Yep, it was bound to happen!" Others just couldn't believe their eyes when they saw the huge plume of flames in the air. The workers who made it to safety ran into town to tell their story, while the other unfortunate individuals in the plant were killed instantly.

Eagle Eye and his warriors rode up to the hilly areas just above the leveled plant and set off to the hydro dam to carry out the next step in their well-organized plan. On the small, dusty road, the warriors met up with Daniel who was on his way to see what had happened. Daniel, taken by surprise by Richard's new appearance, didn't know what to say to his friend. Richard broke the silence.

"I am now of the Yankton tribe, my friend, and the name they have given me is Eagle Eye!"

"What happened down there?" Daniel asked.

"The warriors and I have taken down the nitro plant, and a state of war has been declared upon all of us Yankton because of Rippford's lies," Eagle Eye said.

"You need to stay out of town until this war is over," one of the warriors told Daniel.

"I guess I will!" Daniel said. "Matter of fact, I ain't goin' into town for nuttin'!"

Daniel told Eagle Eye he would probably head up into Hot Springs or Buffalo Gap from there. Eagle Eye and Daniel parted ways not knowing whether they would ever see each other again.

*   *   *   *

At Silver City, the Union Army's train was being serviced while General Slinger told his men about the situation in Creek Canyon. Slinger's plan was, as always, to simply slaughter the Indians. He and his bloodthirsty gang celebrated their mission by tossing their hats in the air and drinking whiskey from their flasks. The train engineer also had a flask of whiskey with him, but for other reasons. Because of his fear of high bridges, the engineer didn't like the high trestle on the train route from Silver City to Creek Canyon. When the train was ready to roll, Slinger and his men boarded the train cars, excited to carry out their orders. The train blew its whistle, and the steam engine began to turn its drive wheels to chug its way up to speed. The Union Army was on the way to do battle with the Yankton.

*   *   *   *

After Eagle Eye met up with Fighting Bear, Crouching Cougar, and the other warriors, they planned to surround the hydro dam and drive out the workers. The warriors shot warning shots with their arrows while they shouted battle cries to startle the workmen. The men at the dam didn't hesitate to arm themselves and fired their guns at the warriors. The warriors, however, were a safe distance from the gunfire in hiding spots. Finally, the workers surrendered after running out of ammunition.

"You men are better off riding into town, before you get yourselves killed!" Eagle Eye shouted to the cowboys.

The workers jumped on their horses and high-tailed it back into Creek Canyon where they thought they could gather up a posse and return to the dam to finish off the tribesmen. The workers first stopped at the telegram office to wire Rapid City about the events taking place at the dam, but when they got there, the telegram operator was nowhere to be found, and the lines were cut.

The warriors under Fighting Bear's command darted across the top of the dam because the water didn't flow over top of the dam. Instead, the water flowed through very large vertical iron tunnels behind the dam and down to underground tunnels leading to the plant. The tunnels also channeled water to other mining operations.

The warriors secured ropes to the tops of the stone supports in front of the dam. Like they had done on the cliffs near the village, the warriors swung back and forth while sliding down the ropes. The men placed sticks of dynamite stolen from the nitro plant onto the stone supports and then ran the ignition wires from each of the bundles of dynamite. Once they were done, they connected the wires to one main line.

Crouching Cougar's warriors ran the roll of the single ignition wire up one side of the cliff the dam was built into. Crouching Cougar passed the ignition wire from one warrior to another until the wire was at the top of the cliff. Then Crouching Cougar attached the wire to the hand-operated detonator, leaving its T-handle in the raised position.

Fighting Bear, Eagle Eye, and the other warriors rejoined Crouching Cougar and his warriors. All eyes were on Eagle Eye as the men waited for him to make the next move.

Eagle Eye placed his foot on the top of the detonator's T-handle. "This is the beginning of the end!" he said.

Eagle Eye pushed the T-handle down with his foot, and in that instant, the bundles of dynamite exploded! The explosion sent pieces of rock, mortar, and dust into the air amid a cloud of black smoke. The thunderous sound of the explosion echoed off the canyon walls. The warriors took cover from the flying debris as they watched the dam's massive stone supports collapse into a big pile of rubble.

The explosion was heard for miles around, even in the town of Creek Canyon. Daniel heard the explosion while en route to Hot Springs and said to himself, "Now, what in tarnation could that be?"

The Creek Canyon townspeople also wondered what was happening, and all they could think was that it was those damn Indians again, trying to disrupt their livelihood.

After the dust and smoke had cleared, Eagle Eye, Fighting Bear, and Crouching Cougar looked down from the cliffs, bewildered at what they saw. The hydro dam was still standing! The three exchanged looks, not knowing what to do next. They had used all the dynamite they had. Crouching Cougar looked at Eagle Eye.

"The Wall of Evil still stands!" he said.

Fighting Bear was also stunned to see the structure still erect and didn't say anything at all.

"That dam should have gone down!" Eagle Eye said.

"What shall we do next?" Fighting Bear asked.

The warriors were silent. Knowing the Union Army was on its way for the slaughter, Eagle Eye finally turned to his companions.

"We have no other choice now but to warn the others of the Army and run to the mountains," he said.

Eagle Eye, Fighting Bear, and Crouching Cougar turned to their warriors and told them to go back to the village and warn those who had stayed behind. The warriors were instructed to have the men, women, and children dismantle the teepees and prepare for a massive exodus to the high mountains of the Black Hills. The warriors obeyed the command and headed back to the village while the three leaders stayed behind.

"We won many battles, but we have lost this war!" said Crouching Cougar. "I do not have much faith in the spirits because I lost my family to the reservoir!"

Eagle Eye couldn't answer his fellow warrior, for even he and Fighting Bear, feeling defeated, were at a loss concerning their faith. They had been victorious in their plans until now, only to be stopped by a giant rock wall!

"Eagle Eye, where are the spirits now? Do they even exist to help us?" Crouching Cougar asked.

Eagle Eye still remained silent.

The three warriors decided to return with the others to help dismantle the village and prepare for their pilgrimage, just as they had when their land was flooded. When they were about to depart from the dam, they suddenly heard a cry echoing off the canyon walls. Eagle Eye, Crouching Cougar, and Fighting Bear looked around a bit before Fighting Bear saw where the shouting was coming from.

"Look! Up there!" Fighting Bear yelled.

The three of them saw the elder of the spiritual leaders crying out a chant to the sky with his hands raised in the air. The spiritual man stood high above the reservoir, up on the rocks while calling out prayers in the Yankton language to the sky. Eagle Eye turned to the other two.

"What is the man saying?" Eagle Eye asked.

"He is crying out to Creator to help free the spirits trapped beneath the waters," Crouching Cougar said. "Silly old man! Creator won't help us now!"

To their surprise, a multitude of cries, chants, singing, and shouting suddenly rang out from behind the elder. All the village's men, women, and children were backing up their spiritual leader! The canyon filled with the sounds of chants and prayers that echoed off the water and the canyon walls. The three warriors stood there, amazed to see such a collection of people.

As the villagers chanted and prayed, Eagle Eye was looking down at a cluster of weeds. Out from under the cluster walked a little spotted sandpiper that looked up at him. It made the same little *peet-tweet-tweet* sound as the one had done to Johnnie back at the ranch.

At that moment, Eagle Eye had a flashback to when his son, Jonathan, was telling him about the Bible story he had learned about in Sunday school back east. It was the story of how Joshua and the children of Israel fought the battle of Jericho. Eagle Eye also remembered explaining to his son about having faith to bring down walls. Eagle Eye paused for a moment, and then he shouted one word to the other two warriors. "*Jericho!*"

"Jericho?" Fighting Bear asked.

"Who is this Jericho?" Crouching Cougar asked.

Eagle Eye didn't answer right away because he was being fulfilled with the renewal of his faith. Eagle Eye shook himself out of his small trance.

"I-I-I'll tell you later. But now, we must go up to the old man and do the same as he is doing! Come! We have no time to spare!"

The three warriors quickly began to make their way to the top of the rocks where the spiritual leader was standing overlooking the reservoir. But before they reached him, they came upon his horse that carried an assortment of instruments and other spiritual objects draped over its blanket. Fighting Bear grabbed a couple of rattles, while Crouching Cougar took hold of a small, handheld drum. Eagle Eye found a ram's horn and removed it from the elder's collection.

The three warriors walked to where the leader and others were chanting to the sky with their hands raised in the air. The elder looked at Fighting Bear, who stood on his left side, and smiled because he had joined him. Crouching Cougar walked up to the spiritual leader's right side. When the faithful old man saw Crouching Cougar, tears began to stream down his weathered face because he was overjoyed to see him joining the group as well.

Eagle Eye stood on the other side of Crouching Cougar as they all chanted to Creator asking him to free the trapped spirits from the depths of the waters. The spiritual leader turned his face back to the sky and chanted loudly. Fighting Bear shook the rattles. Crouching Cougar beat the small drum. Eagle Eye raised the ram's horn to his lips and began blowing it hard and loud. The four of them, along with the villagers, sounded their instruments and cried out to Creator as loudly as they could.

At the base of the hydro dam, a deep low rumble could be heard. The large stones of the dam started pushing forward and the mortar between them began to crumble to the ground. Soon, water started to spurt from between the stones in the dam. Suddenly, all the birds and insects around the dam grew eerily silent. Absolutely nothing could be heard in the area. Just as the silence itself started to pierce the four chanting men, the whole dam suddenly burst wide open and collapsed! The rocks from the structure seemed to explode in all directions.

The billions of tons of water the dam had been holding back were now pushing through the high, narrow walls of the cliffs where the dam had been anchored for years. The large vertical tunnels located behind the dam toppled over in the rushing current. The narrow canyon was engulfed in a raging, powerful flash flood like no one had ever seen. Everything in the floodwater's path, including large boulders, was being swept downstream. As the raging waters grew more powerful, the reservoir emptied itself into the small, narrow canyon. The four Yankton tribesmen and all the villagers stopped chanting to silently watch the waters drain into the canyon. Eagle Eye finally spoke. "Say good-bye to Hell Town!"

*   *   *   *

The Union Army's train was still en route to Creek Canyon. As the train drew closer, the men led by General Slinger were growing more and more excited by Slinger's enthusiasm to slaughter the Indians. All the men were drinking, playing poker, and bragging about ways they were going kill the Yankton tribe's people. The train started to round a bend as it traveled down a narrow passageway between two cliffs, making it impossible to see what lay ahead. The train engineer spotted the sign that read, "Creek Canyon Bridge ahead," and he started to sweat. The engineer took a couple of swigs of whiskey from his flask because he hated this particular bridge.

The bridge was the largest one in the region. It spanned a chasm that was a mile and three-quarters long, and it towered more than three hundred feet high at its midsection. As the train passed the Creek Canyon Bridge sign, Slinger spotted it and yelled out the window at the top of his lungs, "I smell death just a-lying ahead!"

The others laughed and cheered with their fearless leader. The Union train was not the only thing about to arrive at the train trestle. The raging floodwaters were already filling the canyon under the bridge. The rushing water was rising, putting tremendous pressure on the bridges' support beams. The water became so powerful that the timbers supporting the trestle started to creak and pop as trees and other debris wedged against the wooden structure. The waters pressed harder and harder onto the bridge.

The trestle's midsection started bowing as the waters stretched and twisted the supports until they could no longer withstand the flooding. With loud cracking noises, the timbers snapped and broke loose. The trestle's midsection crashed down into the floodwaters, leaving just a portion of the span still erect. Water was splashing everywhere as the broken timbers and sections of the track hit the water! A massive cloud of dust hung in the large open gap of the trestle.

As the train approached the bridge, the engineer grew even more nervous. He chanted under his breath, "I hate bridges! I hate bridges!"

The engineer took one last swig of whiskey. Then just as the train started to cross the remaining portion of the bridge, the engineer noticed the midsection had collapsed! In an instant, he threw on the emergency brake, causing the iron wheels to lock up. Sparks shot out in all directions as the train's wheels slid along the tracks. Slinger and his men all lurched forward.

"What is going on?" they yelled.

One of the soldiers looked out the window and yelled, "The bridge is out! The bridge is out!"

The train skidded toward the collapsed area of the trestle, sparks still shooting out from under its wheels. As the train neared the end, the engineer pressed himself to the wall inside the cab, frozen with fear. The train came to a halt just before it was about to go over the edge.

"Back this thing up!" the men yelled. "Back this thing up!"

The engineer snapped out of his state of shock and was shivering all over. His body was drenched with sweat. The engineer threw the control lever into reverse, and the big, iron drive wheels started to spin backward in an attempt to back the train off the bridge. While the train started to chug in reverse, the weakened timbers started to twist and crack under its weight. Ever so slowly, as the train backed up, the timbers started splitting. The men had no way of getting off of the train. The only way off the train was to back it off the bridge or to plummet hundreds of feet through the canyon to the floodwaters below. The train picked up speed in reverse, and the men cheered.

"Come on, mister! Get this thing off this bridge 'cause we got some killing to do!" they yelled.

The train crept backward as the timbers continued to split and buckle under the weight. Just before the caboose reached the end of the bridge, the timbers could no longer withstand the train's weight and gave out. With one big crash, the trestle collapsed, and the train plunged toward the bottom of the canyon. As the train made its descent, it smashed through the crisscrossed timbers that had supported the trestle. The bridge's beams pierced the wooden cars, tearing them to shreds before the cars even hit the canyon walls. One large, splintered beam went through the window where General Slinger was standing and ripped right through his chest!

The heavy iron train engine was first to crash into the walls of the canyon. When it hit, the steam pressure caused the engine to explode everywhere. The wooden train cars also broke apart as they crashed down the sloping, rocky walls of the canyon. The steel wheels from the train cars ricochet in all directions as they fell. Finally, as the train's parts and its victims reached the canyon's bottom, they slid into the rushing waters along with the bridge supports.

*   *   *   *

At the reservoir, Eagle Eye, Fighting Bear, and Crouching Cougar gave the instruments back to the spiritual man and jumped on their horses. They rode along the canyon's upper rim, following the floodwater's path of destruction. The elderly spiritual man headed back to the village with the others to celebrate. The villagers were overjoyed that the trapped spirits had been finally released. As they rode their horses to the mountains, the Yankton people sang chants of victory, thanking Creator for helping the trapped spirits start their journey home. The villagers were overjoyed at the dam's collapse because it meant they might not have to flee to the mountains after all.

Eagle Eye, Fighting Bear, and Crouching Cougar first came upon the railroad trestle that was nothing but a pile of splintered timbers floating in the water. The warriors also saw pieces of the Union Army's train that had been smashed upon the cliff walls. Then they galloped to their last destination, Creek Canyon.

In town, the men of Creek Canyon were planning attacks led by the sheriff. Sheriff Rippford rounded up more men who had been oppressing

Richard DuFour from the very beginning. The sheriff and his newly appointed deputies set off to form posses to help aid the Union Army. Saloons were packed with bloodthirsty men drinking whiskey and hooting and hollering about what they planned to do to the Yankton people.

While the drunken men were carrying on with their evil business, they didn't hear the bottles of liquor on the shelves clink together when the ground started to shake. The rattling grew louder and louder as the ground's rumbling grew more powerful. The saloon became eerily quiet as all the men stopped their boisterous behavior. Even the music from the player pianos stopped. Everyone looked at one another and wondered where the rumbling was coming from. The floor began to vibrate, and the building's walls began to shake. Liquor bottles fell off the shelves, and the oil lamps suspended from the ceilings swayed back and forth. "Earthquake!" the townspeople yelled.

People rushed out into the streets to avoid the buildings collapsing on them, only to realize it wasn't an earthquake after all. What the townspeople saw sent them running in all directions. A great wall of water was rushing down the canyon right toward the town! As the wall of water approached them, it was pushing an assortment of trees, mud, and debris from the fallen bridge faster than any horse could run!

The sheriff was in the jailhouse office at the time when he and the jail keeper saw the great flood coming toward them. Both men bolted toward a ladder leading to the rooftop, leaving the prisoners behind to fend for themselves. The jailer got to the ladder before the sheriff did and started to climb as fast as he could. However, the jail keeper was heavyset and old.

"Hurry up, old man!" the sheriff yelled. "If you weren't so damn fat, you'd be up there by now!"

In a panic, Sheriff Rippford pulled out one of his pistols and shot the jail keeper in the back, sending his body plummeting to the floor.

Appalled prisoners were frantically yelling, "Let us out of here, Sheriff! Let us out of here!"

Ignoring the prisoners' cries, Rippford stepped on the jail keeper's body to climb the ladder to save his own skin. The cowardly sheriff made his way through a hatch in the roof and stood up on the rooftop just in time to witness the events taking place in his own town.

Giant walls of muddy water were smashing through the buildings. As the people in the streets tried to outrun the mighty waters, they were quickly swept away, right off their feet, and consumed in the rapid current. Those who took refuge on rooftops found themselves floating downstream on broken beams of wood that served as nothing more than rickety rafts. The clapboard buildings that had once sheltered them from sun, wind, and rain had been washed away by the water's force. Anyone inside the buildings could do nothing but watch the walls crash inward from the ferocious floodwaters.

No one in town that day could escape the fierce currents. Every building in town was swept away. Anyone who tried to flee to higher ground found himself trapped against the base of the narrow canyon walls. The rock walls made it impossible for anyone to climb them fast enough to escape the rapidly rising waters. However, one building still stood—the jailhouse constructed of stone. The floodwaters had pushed the windows in and drowned the prisoners inside, but the sheriff remained on the building's roof.

Eagle Eye and his two fellow warriors arrived at the site where the town once stood and saw the sheriff on top of the jailhouse. The three of them said nothing. The sheriff soon spotted the three warriors high above him. Sheriff Rippford yelled, "Save me! Save me!"

Eagle Eye, Crouching Cougar, and Fighting Bear watched the sheriff frantically pacing back and forth on the rooftop.

"Come on, you damn Injuns!" the sheriff shouted at them.

Then, as the water pressure increased against the walls of the jailhouse, the sheriff felt the building shudder under his feet. Still silently looking on, the three warriors watched as the cowardly sheriff performed his last act as a so-called law-man. He pulled out his pistols and wildly shot toward Eagle Eye, Fighting Bear, and Crouching Cougar. The bullets had no chance of hitting the three warriors as Rippford demonstrated one last stint of cowardliness.

The jailhouse proved to be no match against the floodwaters, and it gave way. As the jail sank into the water, the rooftop buckled, and the sheriff realized his own fate. As Rippford went down with the sinking roof, he yelled out one last cry to the warriors.

"*You traaaaaders!*"

The sheriff sank below the water's surface. The only thing the men saw again of Sheriff Rippford was his hat floating on top of the water.

The debris from the jailhouse and the other buildings rushed farther down the canyon and came to a very high cliff. The floodwaters swept their contents over the cliff, and everything crashed to the bottom. Creek Canyon, otherwise known as "Hell Town," no longer existed.

Eagle Eye, Fighting Bear, and Crouching Cougar turned their horses around and slowly rode back toward the village. As the three warriors rode into the mountains, an American bald eagle flew high above them and screeched.

It didn't take long for the news of Creek Canyon's destruction to reach Rapid City. Headlines in large print covered front pages of newspapers saying,

Dam Break Destroys Creek Canyon!
All Perish!!

Inside the pages of the newspapers, many articles explained how the hydro dam burst and first destroyed the train trestle and then the town of Creek Canyon. The news reported that all who lived in Creek Canyon were swept away and drowned. The residents of Rapid City were surprised by another report in the newspapers that said a well-informed telegram operator had tipped off government officials about the Creek Canyon sheriff's plot to kill Indians for money instead of relocating them.

Everyone in Rapid City was stunned by the news. They shook their heads in disgust over the deaths of Creek Canyon's residents.

That is, of course, everyone except for one young Yankton waitress. She smiled.

www.ingramcontent.com/pod-product-compliance
Lightning Source LLC
Chambersburg PA
CBHW071017120626
46546CB00003B/1131